Reading Texts |

"Signs are never innocent. Semiotics
teaches us that."

"Semi-what?"

David Lodge, *Nice Work*

Danuta Fjellestad
Eleanor Wikborg

Reading Texts
An Introduction to Strategies of Interpretation

SCANDINAVIAN UNIVERSITY PRESS
Oslo – Stockholm – Copenhagen – Boston

Scandinavian University Press (Universitetsforlaget AS)
P.O. Box 2959 Tøyen, N-0608 Oslo, Norway
Fax +47 22 57 53 53

Stockholm office
SCUP, Scandinavian University Press
P.O. Box 3255, S-103 65 Stockholm, Sweden
Fax +46 8 20 99 82

Copenhagen office
Scandinavian University Press AS
P.O. Box 54, DK-1002 København K, Denmark
Fax +45 33 32 05 70

Boston office
Scandinavian University Press North America
875 Massachusetts Ave., Ste. 84, Cambridge MA 02139, USA
Fax +1 617 354 6875

© Scandinavian University Press (Universitetsforlaget AS), Oslo 1995

ISBN 82-00-22696-4

Design: Astrid Elisabeth Jørgensen
Typeset in 10.5 on 13 point Photina by HS-Repro A/S
Printed on 90 g Partner Offset by HS-Trykk A/S, Norway 1995

For our students –
past, present, and future

Contents

Unit One:

The process of decoding cultural texts 1
The aim of the exercises in this unit is to make you aware
that processes of decoding are a part of your everyday experience. The unit introduces the concepts of a sign, cultural
codes, and binary oppositions, which often organize cultural codes. We discuss combinations of codes in terms of
their appeal to the emotions for purposes of persuasion.

Material:
    color circles
    a family portrait
    cigarette advertisements
    a sequence of Marilyn Monroe pictures

Unit Two:

**The rhetoric of reporting and persuasion in
newspaper texts** 7
The aim of the exercises in this unit is to have you investi-
gate the issue of persuasion in newspaper texts by examining the complex interaction of fact and opinion in the type
of newspaper article that combines reporting with argu-
mentation.

Material:

Jerry Adler et al., excerpt from "Thought Police,"
Newsweek
William Safire, "'Correct Thinking' on the Campus,"
International Herald Tribune

Unit Three:

The rhetoric of reporting and persuasion
in history texts
In this unit, which looks at how three historians describe
Abraham Lincoln, we continue our analysis of the various
ways in which even the most apparently objective texts convey a point of view. We also explore the links between history and other types of text.

Material:

Herbert Agar, excerpt from *The Price of Union*
John Garraty, excerpt from *The American Nation*
Howard Zinn, excerpt from *A People's History of the
United States*

Unit Four:

Literature and "reality": the role of genre
expectations
The aim of the exercises in this unit is to show both the
necessity of literal reading for verisimilitude and the tensions between such "obvious" readings and less obvious
or "metaphorical" ones. We also discuss how genre conventions establish powerful "horizons of expectations" in
reading.

Material:

Katherine Mansfield, "A Suburban Fairy Tale"
William Carlos Williams, "This Is Just to Say"
Sylvia Plath, "Mushrooms"

In this unit we address the issues of gender and race in textual representation and in the interpretation of texts. The questions about "A Rose for Emily" (Section One) and about the excerpts from "Benito Cereno" and *Sula* (Section Two) are designed to draw your attention to elements in the stories that relate to the issues involved in representing gender and race. The questions on the critical pieces are aimed at getting you to consider what it means to read a text from a gender- or ethnic-specific position.

Material:
William Faulkner, "A Rose for Emily"
Cleanth Brooks and Robert Penn Warren, excerpt from
    Understanding Fiction
Robert Crosman, excerpt from "How Readers Make
    Meaning"
Judith Fetterley, excerpts from *The Resisting Reader*
Herman Melville, excerpts from "Benito Cereno"
Toni Morrison, excerpt from *Sula*

In this unit we consider some of the ways in which texts make use of other texts through, for instance, pastiche, quotation, or allusion. We illustrate these techniques with three paintings. We then read the "Friday" texts for their ideological dimensions and reflect on the role of the reader's familiarity with the "parent text" in the process of interpretation.

Material:
Marcel Duchamp, *Mona Lisa: L.H.O.O.Q.*
Ferdinand Léger, *Mona Lisa with Keys*
René Magritte, *The Gioconda*
Daniel Defoe, excerpt from *Robinson Crusoe*
J. M. Coetzee, excerpt from *Foe*

Unit Seven:

The unit introduces you to certain concepts which are used in the study of narrative. Then we turn to film versions of the two novels in order to examine how a literary text can be presented in a medium which has a different narrative form.

Material:
> F. Scott Fitzgerald, opening pages from *The Great Gatsby*
> *The Great Gatsby*, opening scenes from Jack Clayton's film
> John Fowles, opening pages from *The French Lieutenant's Woman*
> *The French Lieutenant's Woman*, opening scenes from Karel Reisz's film

Unit Eight:

The exercises in this unit introduce you to some of the interpretive constraints currently operating in criticism. We discuss the question of acceptability and the "correctness" of interpretation in the context of various interpretive theories or reading paradigms.

Material:
> William Wordsworth, "A Slumber Did My Spirit Seal ..."
> F. W. Bateson, excerpt from *English Poetry*
> Cleanth Brooks, excerpt from "Irony as a Principle of Structure"
> J. Hillis Miller, excerpts from *Romanticism and Contemporary Criticism*
> Emily Dickinson, "My Life had stood – a Loaded Gun –"
> Charles R. Anderson, excerpts from *Emily Dickinson's Poetry: Stairway of Surprise*
> Albert Gelpi, excerpt from "Emily Dickinson and the Deerslayer"

Adrienne Rich, excerpt from "Vesuvius at Home:
  The Poetry of Emily Dickinson"
Shira Wolosky, excerpt from *Emily Dickinson: A Voice
  of War*

Unit Nine:

The question of value... 134
In this unit we consider some of the ways in which our culture attributes value to literary texts. We look at selected
texts in the contexts of various cultural "institutions" and
"reading communities." We reflect especially on the ideological function of such labels as "high culture" and "low
(or mass) culture."

Material:
  Joseph Conrad, excerpt from *Heart of Darkness*
  William Faulkner, excerpt from *Absalom, Absalom!*
  Margaret Mitchell, excerpt from *Gone with the Wind*
  Edgar Rice Burroughs, excerpt from *Tarzan of the Apes*

Acknowledgments

This book has grown out of a course which we taught and developed over a three-year period. We start, therefore, by thanking our students for cheerfully putting up with even our wilder flights of experimentation. Their probing questions and insightful answers have influenced this book in countless ways.

We also extend heartfelt thanks to colleagues and friends who have read various parts of the manuscript – for their enthusiastic encouragement, their vigorous opposition, and their generous attention to detail: Helga Drougge, Helena Eriksson, Rolf Lundén, Erik Löfroth (Uppsala University); Sheila Ghose, Steven Hartman, Alan McMillion, David Minugh, Catherine Sandbach Dahlström (Stockholm University); Lennart Nyberg and Marianne Thormählen (Lund University), and Mall Stålhammar (Göteborg University).

Finally, our special thanks go to Anne Bindslev of Scandinavian University Press, whose unfailing trust in the project and practical advice in matters great and small helped us through a number of difficult moments.

Dear Student

The decisions of our everyday lives depend on a multitude of interpretive gestures: whenever we cross the street, take a train or bus,
or decide what to eat at a restaurant, we unconsciously pick up
signs which we make sense of by means of codes that give those
signs meaning. In fact, any living organism's survival depends on
its recognition and interpretation of meaningful signs. To perceive
is to categorize and classify in terms of a systematization of experience which involves an impressive range of interpretive strategies.

But how similar is the decoding of, for example, signs to find
your way to the "right" toilet to the decoding of cultural artifacts?
As we hope to show, there may be a difference in complexity, but
basically the activities are the same. Let us consider this question
in relation to a scene from David Lodge's *Nice Work*, which drama-
tizes an encounter between Robyn Penrose, a university teacher
of English, and Victor Wilcox, an industrial managing director.
At one point they discuss an advertisement for a cigarette brand
called Silk Cut. The ad is described as "a photographic depiction of
a rippling expanse of purple silk in which there was a single slit, as
if the material had been slashed with a razor. There were no words
on the advertisement, except for the Government Health Warning
about smoking." Intrigued by this picture, Robyn Penrose offers
an analysis of the ad. In her reading, "[t]he shimmering silk, with
its voluptuous curves and sensuous texture, obviously symbolized
the female body, and the elliptical slit, foregrounded by a lighter
colour showing through, was still more obviously a vagina. The

advert thus appealed to both sensual and sadistic impulses, the desire to mutilate as well as penetrate the female body." Victor Wilcox reacts to Robyn's interpretation with outrage and disbelief:

> "You must have a twisted mind to see all that in a perfectly harmless bit of cloth," he said.
>
> "What's the point of it, then?" Robyn challenged him. "Why use cloth to advertise cigarettes?"
>
> "Well, that's the name of 'em, isn't it? Silk Cut. It's a picture of the name. Nothing more or less."
>
> "Suppose they'd used a picture of a roll of silk cut in half – would that do just as well?"
>
> "I suppose so. Yes, why not?"
>
> "Because it would look like a penis cut in half, that's why."
>
> He forced a laugh to cover his embarrassment. "Why can't you people take things at their face value?"
>
> "What people are you referring to?"
>
> "Highbrows. Intellectuals. You're always trying to find hidden meanings in things. Why? A cigarette is a cigarette. A piece of silk is a piece of silk. Why not leave it at that?"
>
> "When they're represented they acquire additional meanings," said Robyn. "Signs are never innocent. Semiotics teaches us that."
>
> "Semi-what?"
>
> "Semiotics. The study of signs." (p. 220–21)

What is your response to Robyn Penrose's reading of the "deep structure" or "hidden meaning" of the Silk Cut advertisement? Do you side with Victor Wilcox's dismissal of her interpretation? Why should the ad's hidden meaning be "obvious" to the teacher but totally obscure to the manager?

Questions of this kind will be a starting point in our discussions of how signs signify in our culture. This book is meant to help you understand, reflect on, and question the processes of interpretation – your own, that of your classmates, and that of the academic community of which you are a member. Its focus is not so much on what texts mean as on how meanings are textually constructed and how they are then critically reconstructed.

The conversation between Robyn and Vic indicates that texts may be read (interpreted) in a number of ways. Vic's understanding of the ad in terms of "it means what it says" may be called commonsensical; Robyn's reading, as a literary scholar would recognize, is informed by the insights of feminist theory in its psychoanalytic orientation. In other words, the difference in Robyn's and Vic's understanding of the ad may be explained by the fact that they employ different interpretive paradigms. The concept of commonsense is familiar to you; as for literary theory you may or may not have been exposed to the modes of thinking of which Robyn's interpretation is an example. In this book we would like to take a closer look at "commonsense" and to introduce you to some of the issues raised by contemporary theory.

Let us consider "commonsense" first. Today it is believed that the notion of "commonsense" is, as Catherine Belsey has expressed it,

> ideologically and discursively constructed, rooted in a specific historical situation and operating in conjunction with a particular social formation. In other words, it is argued that what seems obvious and natural is not necessarily so, but that on the contrary the "obvious" and the "natural" are not given but produced in a specific society by the ways in which that society talks and thinks about itself and its experience. (p. 3)

One of the goals of the exercises in this book is to help you become aware of the cultural conditioning of your own commonsense, since your expectations, assumptions, and beliefs play an important role in your interpretation of various texts. You will notice that most of our exercises begin with a suggestion that you jot down your initial response to the text studied. We would like to encourage you to keep a journal (record) of your "first impressions" in order that you may be able to examine them critically. Self-awareness helps, we believe, in arguing interpretations, in clarifying misunderstandings, and in examining one's views.

Although you are an individual reader with your own temperament and tastes, your response to texts is also a cultural phenomenon; that is, as a reader of a given age, gender, class, nationality, and educational background, to a considerable degree you are a product and carrier of the assumptions and beliefs of your culture. Awareness of this cultural heritage and "conditioning" makes it possible to resist manipulation and exploitation by, for instance, the mass media.

Contemporary literary theory sees reading and making sense

of signs as a *situated* activity. That is, interpretation is perceived as time- and culture-bound. Interpretive skills are also institutional skills; that is, the institutions like the one at which you are taking the course hold a more or less general consensus regarding what is expected of a good, convincing interpretation. We want to help you acquire such skills. We want to introduce you to some of the conventions that are accepted in academia. The most important of these is the ability to adduce convincing textual evidence. Whatever assertions you make about the text, they are expected to be supported by references to specific elements in the text. The most perceptive analysis attempts to link various aspects of the text. As the famous semiotician Umberto Eco points out, "any interpretation given of a certain portion of a text can be accepted if it is confirmed by, and must be rejected if it is challenged by, another portion of the text. In this sense the internal textual coherence controls the otherwise uncontrollable drives of the reader" (p. 65).

Raising questions rather than providing answers is the key aim of this book. The book is not meant to give you definite answers about the meaning of its chosen texts; its intention is to encourage you to ask questions and to reflect on your answers. At times you may be frustrated and tired of all this questioning and yearn for a state of certainty and definite knowledge, for the world of "correct" answers. We do not believe in providing this security; we believe instead that the questioning will help you emerge as an empowered scholar.

Indeed, we would like you to use whatever doubts or objections you may feel as you work your way through the material in this book as fuel in your intellectual development. You may not always want to voice your dissent in the classroom. For this reason we recommend that you keep a journal or record of your queries and objections. You may then want to discuss them with your teacher in an individual conference, or you may eventually choose to voice them in class. And you are always welcome to write to us; we promise to answer your letters as best we can.

On the cover of the book you have seen two names which you have identified as the "authors." Since this is a textbook, you have probably assumed that we – the authors – are teachers. But we have had a number of co-authors whose names do not appear on the cover. These are our students whom we have taught over many years. It was our students' questions, their comments on the texts we discussed, and their insights that inspired us to write this book.

Yours,
Danuta Fjellestad and Eleanor Wikborg

Unit One

The process of decoding cultural texts

The aim of the exercises in this unit is to make you aware of the processes of interpretation that are a part of our everyday experience. The unit introduces the concepts of a sign, binary oppositions, and codes. These terms are generally used in semiotics, that is, the study of the processes of communication, expression, and representation.

So let us start:

EXERCISE 1: COLOR CIRCLES

1. Draw three colored circles, yellow, red, and green, on separate pieces of paper. Please arrange these circles in *any way you want to*, but be prepared to account for your arrangement. Try to think of the possible "meaning" of any *one* of these colors in contexts other than that of your arrangement. (*Note*: The notions of "correct" and "incorrect" and "good" and "bad" are not applicable here; the only point is that you be aware of your "organizing principle.")
2. Listen carefully to your own and others' justifications of the different arrangements. Do you and your classmates defend them by appeals to emotions? ideas? rules? Whose emotions, ideas, or rules? Do you all share these emotions, ideas, or rules?

The purpose of comparing your own answers to the task with the answers given by your fellow students is not to decide who is wrong and who is right, but to observe how we go about justifying our different interpretations. You may notice that you are more willing to accept some interpretations than others. You may also notice that some arrangements need to be explained in detail before they begin to "mean" something to you, while the meaning of others appears to be "obvious" and in need of no (or little) explanation. This second kind of arrangement is usually grounded in systems of thought and regulations which are shared by many (indeed, often all) members of a given community.

The next exercise illustrates how the "same" sign may acquire different meanings in different contexts and how different signs may mean the "same" thing.

EXERCISE 2: "LADIES" (SEE P. 187)

1. Jot down possible meanings of the word *ladies.*
2. Now arrange the enclosed signs in pairs and columns. In which of the columns would you place *ladies?* Can you think of a context in which the signs in each column would mean the same thing? That is, in what context would the "pictures" have the same meaning?

The concept of a "sign" as defined by the Swiss linguist Ferdinand de Saussure (1857–1913) is important to both the theory and the practice of semiotics. In his view a sign is the union of a phonic or graphic element (called a "signifier") with a concept (a "signified"). The word *rose,* for example, would be a signifier that is linked with several possible signifieds (e.g. a species of flower, beauty, love, etc.). Saussure saw signs as acquiring specific meanings within a given system or context. Within such systems signs are seen as oppositional and relational. To take an example from the "faucet code," the signifier *red* means "hot water" in opposition (and in relation) to *blue,* which signals "cold water."

Let us consider the sign *queen.* If you were asked what the signifier *queen* meant to you, you might mention several concepts, or signifieds, depending on the system in which you situated the sign. You might think of *queen* in opposition to *king,* hence a royal consort. Alternatively, you might think of a chess or bridge game.

In each of the systems, the sign *queen* stands in opposition to other signs; in each, it is related to them in a specific way. For instance, the power position of *queen* is different in chess than in bridge. Unless we know the rules of chess (or other games with the figure of the queen), we will not be able to assign the piece called *queen* its position in the system. Simply put, in that case we will not know what *queen* "means."

In the three exercises below we examine how different combinations of signs in various codes operate in order to stir emotions, attract attention, or persuade.

EXERCISE 3: A FAMILY PORTRAIT (SEE P. 189)

This picture was exhibited in the photography section of the Museum of Modern Art in Stockholm. This means that it is presented as a work of art. There is a considerable difference between looking at a picture of your own family members, or of people you know, and looking at a *representation* of a family as a concept, which is the case here.

1. Take a look at the photograph. What features in it would you pick out as justifying its title, *An Ordinary Family*? In other words, what signs of the "family code" would you pick out? Consider such elements as the relative size and position of the people in the photograph, their clothing, and the setting in which the group is presented.
2. Now look for the features which in your opinion make the family in the photograph different from an ordinary "mother–father–child" group. In the light of the differences, how would you explain the effect of the title?
3. Consider the composition of the photograph and look for signals of its "artiness."

EXERCISE 4: CARTIER, MARLBORO, AND DUNHILL ADS
(SEE PP. 190–91)

Note: For copyright reasons the publisher was unable to provide you with a reproduction of a Marlboro ad. You will easily find the ad in one of its many variants in such magazines as *Time* and *Newsweek*.

1. Take a *quick* look at the Cartier, Marlboro, and Dunhill advertisements and immediately jot down the "message" that these ads seem to be sending. Write down also your first, emotional response to the ads.
2. Now analyze each ad in turn, paying attention to as much detail as possible. Pay attention to each ad's use of colors and lines, and its general composition. You may find the following terms useful: balance, contrast, dynamism, tension, symmetry, asymmetry, repetition, harmony, juxtaposition, simplicity, regularity, sharpness, instability, warmth, coolness, richness, poverty, nature, culture.
3. Now take another look at the ads and try to decide who their addressees may be: everybody? men? women? children? Can you characterize the receivers in some detail?
4. Do you see any connection between the visual and the emotional messages of the ads?
5. Read the caption for each ad: what messages do the captions send? In what way are they (or are they not) congruent with the visual messages?
6. Once again try to decide the addressees of each ad. Do your earlier answers still hold? On what grounds would you defend or dismiss them?

EXERCISE 5: THE MARILYN MONROE PICTURES (SEE P. 192)

1. Take a look at the three pictures and select the one you find most amusing. What is it in the picture that appeals to you?
2. What do the three pictures have in common? Try to identify both the various compositional elements and their arrangement.

3. What oppositions (tensions) do you see in the pictures?
4. Identify the focalization in the pictures; that is, try to see who is looking at what/whom. Where do you stand as an observer? Does your focus coincide with that of any of the viewers in the pictures?

You will probably agree that various texts – be they books, pictures, or films – need to be interpreted. However, you may not have reflected on the fact that to order a meal, to shop, or to participate in a discussion, you have to "decode" or interpret a number of signs. Your success or failure in such everyday activities depends on such decoding, which is mostly a subconscious process. The exercises in this unit are meant to bring some instances of this subconscious process to your consciousness.

As you may have already noticed, we can distinguish between private, idiosyncratic codes (or principles of interpretation) and codes which are shared by a larger community. You may have noticed, too, that it is easier to reach a consensus about the meaning of a given text if interpretive codes are shared and interpretation is not grounded in idiosyncratic associations. In other words, interpretations anchored in community (cultural) codes tend to be accepted as "correct." Interpretations governed by idiosyncratic codes are less readily accepted. We could say that if codes are shared, the process of communication is smoother than if they are not.

Certain texts, most notably commercials of all kinds, rely heavily on the receivers' subconscious knowledge of cultural coding. The moment of surprise that many commercials and ads employ often depends on unusual combinations of certain codes. For example, in an ad for Absolut vodka, the bottle is shown resting at the bottom of the sea with goldfish swimming around. The ad is composed on the principle of the clash of two worlds: alcohol, a beverage manufactured by and for human beings, is placed in an "alien" context of nature; fish can neither swim in nor drink this "transformed" water. (The ad's coding is much more complex, of course; you may want to explore it further.)

We want to stress, however, that although the concepts of codes, coding, and decoding are very useful in interpretation, they also have their limitations. Meanings and "messages" of various texts can seldom be exhaustively explained by citing a few – or even a great many – codes. It is very important to remember too that codes do not exist "out there" in nature or reality, but are socially and culturally constructed and thus subject to change. We will return to this issue in later units.

WRITTEN ASSIGNMENTS

1. Find an example of an ad or a commercial to which you have a strong response (be it surprise, amusement, confusion) and try to explain what in the ad evoked your initial reaction.
2. Look through a newspaper or a magazine with which you are well acquainted and find an ad which leaves you indifferent. How do you explain the ad's failure to arouse your interest?

See "Binary oppositions," "Code," "Model of communication," and "Text" in the Glossary.

Unit Two

The rhetoric of reporting and persuasion in newspaper texts

The texts we have chosen for this unit are two expository newspaper articles. Both articles aim to be surveys of a cultural phenomenon while at the same time they openly express opinions. As surveys, they aspire to journalistic standards of objectivity. Despite such standards, however, the various rhetorical strategies to which the exercises draw attention have the effect, as we shall see, of persuading the reader to adopt a certain point of view.

Material:

> Jerry Adler et al., excerpt from "Thought Police," *Newsweek*, January 14, 1991
>
> William Safire, "'Correct Thinking' on the Campus," *International Herald Tribune*, May 6, 1991

EXERCISE 1

Before you read the texts below, make a note of
1. the kind of articles you expect to find in a quality newspaper or news magazine?
2. the ways in which you expect a newspaper article to be different from a piece of fiction, such as a short story. (Journalists, as you know, also talk about their "stories.")

Now read the two articles and answer the questions that follow.

Note: The first text (from *Newsweek*) is an excerpt, the first two pages of a seven-page article. (You will find it easier to read the text reproduced below the magazine layout.) The second text (from the *International Herald Tribune*) reproduces the complete original. We shall treat both texts as units in their own right.

NEWSWEEK, January 14, 1991, Scott Menchin.

Jerry Adler et al.: "Thought Police"

Is this the new enlightenment on campus or the new McCarthyism?

Perhaps Nina Wu, a sophomore at the University of Connecticut, actually didn't like gays. More likely, she thought she was being funny when she allegedly put up a sign on the door to her dorm room listing "people who are shot on sight" – among them, "preppies," "bimbos," "men without chest hair" and "homos." No protests were heard from representatives of the first three categories, but UConn's gay community was more forthright in asserting its prerogatives. Wu was brought up on charges of violating the student-behavior code, which had recently been rewritten to prohibit "posting or advertising publicly offensive, indecent or abusive matter concerning persons ... and making personal slurs or epithets based on race, sex, ethnic origin, disability, religion or sexual orientation." Found guilty last year in a campus administrative hearing, Wu was ... what would you guess? Reprimanded? Ordered to write a letter of apology? No, Wu was ordered to move off campus and forbidden to set foot in any university dormitories or cafeterias. Only under pressure of a federal lawsuit did the university let her move back onto campus this year – and revise the Code of Student Conduct to make it conform to a higher code, the First Amendment.

There is an experiment of sorts taking place in American colleges. Or, more accurately, hundreds of experiments at different campuses, directed at changing the consciousness of this entire generation of university students. The goal is to eliminate prejudice, not just of the petty sort that shows up on sophomore dorm walls, but the grand prejudice that has ruled American universities since their founding: that the intellectual tradition of Western Europe occupies the central place in the history of civilization. In this context it would not be enough for a student to refrain from insulting homosexuals or other minorities. He or she would be expected to "affirm" their presence on campus and to study their literature and culture alongside that of Plato, Shakespeare and Locke. This agenda is broadly shared by most organizations of minority students, feminists and gays. It is also the program of a generation of campus radicals who grew up in the '60s and are now achieving positions of academic influence. If they no longer talk of taking to the streets, it is because they now are gaining access to the conventional weapons of campus politics: social pressure, academic perks (including tenure) and – when they have the administration on their side – outright coercion.

There is no conspiracy at work here, just a creed, a set of beliefs and expressions which students from places as diverse as Sarah Lawrence and San Francisco State recognize instantly as "PC" – politically correct. Plunk down a professor from Princeton, say, in the University of Wisconsin at Madison, show him a student in a tie-dyed T shirt, with open-toed sandals and a grubby knapsack dangling a student-union-issue, environmentally sound, reusable red plastic cup, and he'll recognize the type instantly. It's

"PC Person," an archetype that has now been certified in the official chronicles of American culture, the comic pages. Jeff Shesol, a student cartoonist at Brown, created him as an enforcer of radical cant, so sensitive to potential slights that he even knows the correct euphemism for 9-year-old "girls." He calls them "pre-women."

That is appalling, or would be if it were true. What happened to Nina Wu is in fact appalling, as the university itself seems to have admitted. But so was the incident that led UConn to prohibit "personal slurs" in the first place: a group of white students taunting and spitting at Asian-American students on their way to a dance. If women, gays and racial minorities are seeking special protections, it is because they have been the objects of special attacks. (According to sociologist Howard Ehrlich, each year one minority student in five experiences "ethnoviolent attack," including verbal assaults.) If African-Americans are challenging the primacy of Western civilization, it is because for centuries they were oppressed by it. The oppressed have no monopoly on truth. But surely they have earned the right to critique the society that enslaved them.

The content of PC is, in some respects, uncontroversial: who would *defend* racism? What is distressing is that at the university, of all places, tolerance has to be imposed rather than taught, and that "progress" so often is just the replacement of one repressive orthodoxy by another.

Shelf struggle: The march of PC across American campuses has hardly been unopposed. On the contrary, it has provoked the most extreme reaction, from heartfelt defenses of the First Amendment to the end-of-the-world angst of a Rabelais scholar whose subject has just been dropped from the freshman lit course in favor of Toni Morrison. Opponents of PC now have their own organization, the National Association of Scholars (based in Princeton, N.J.), "committed to rational discourse as the foundation of academic life." It is supported mostly by conservative foundations, but its 1,400 members include some prominent liberals such as Duke political scientist James David Barber, former chair of Amnesty International USA. Duke is a microcosm of the struggle over PC, which is being fought right down to the shelves in the campus bookstore, and not always entirely by rational discourse. Barber stalked into the political-science section one day last spring and turned on its spine every volume with "Marx" in its title – about one out of seven by his count, a lot more attention than he thought it warrants – and angrily demanded their removal. His attempt to organize an NAS chapter at Duke touched off a battle with the influential head of the English department, Stanley Fish, which was extreme even by academic standards of vitriol. Fish called NAS, and by implication its members, "racist, sexist and homophobic." "That," notes one of Barber's allies, "is like calling someone a communist in the McCarthy years."

Opponents of PC see themselves as a beleaguered minority among barbarians who would ban Shakespeare because he didn't write in Swahili.

EXERCISE 2

Read "Thought Police" carefully and then work through the following tasks and questions:

1. Study the layout of the page, which serves as a frame for the article. Starting with the choice of headline, what would you say is its effect on the reader? What contribution is made by its size? Take a look also at the two alternatives presented in the lead ("the new enlightenment ... or the new McCarthyism?"); what is the effect of the order in which they are arranged? Similarly, comment on the purpose of the picture, and of the quote from the article enlarged on the right.

   The placing of articles (and hence their classification) in newspapers and magazines is also of interest. In *Newsweek,* "Back of the Book" is the section toward the end of the magazine which deals with broad cultural issues under such headings as Books, Music, Art, and Education. Does classifying the article under Education add to the overall effect of the other features of its framing enumerated above?

2. The author could have started his article with paragraph 2. Why do you think he chose instead to start with the case of Nina Wu? What difference would it have made if her name had been Betsy Jones?

3. In the first two sentences of paragraph 1, what attitudes would you say are conveyed by the three adverbs "perhaps," "actually," and "allegedly"? Similarly, in the fifth sentence (beginning "Found guilty ...") what is the purpose of the ellipsis, the reference to "you" and the three questions?

4. In paragraph 2, comment on the effect of the quotation marks placed around "affirm," and on the writer's choice of the term "grand prejudice" (which is also given prominence in the high-

6, 1991

LANGUAGE

'Correct Thinking' on the Campus

By William Safire

WASHINGTON — What does "PC" stand for? If your impulse is to blurt out "personal computer," you have gone software in the head. If those letters evoke memories of the Peace Corps, you are antediluvian. A percentage of postcards from hypochondriacs will insist that the initials stand for the Latin direction *post cibum,* "after meals," the only digestively conducive time to pop certain pills.

Those of us with slanguistic *Fingerspitzengefühl,* however, know that the initials stand for the most controversial phrase on college campuses today: *politically correct.* In "Thatch," a comic strip by Jeff Shesol of Brown University, a heroic character slips on a cape and supermanly tights with "PC" emblazoned on his chest. It's not a nerd, it's not a plane, it's . . . Politically Correct Person!

"There is a new McCarthyism that has spread over American college campuses," writes Max Lerner, an old-line liberal. "We call it 'political correctness.'" The new Random House Webster's College Dictionary defines the term as "marked by or adhering to a typically progressive orthodoxy on issues involving especially race, gender, sexual affinity or ecology."

I would edit that definition to denote *politically correct* as "an adverbially premodified adjectival lexical unit used to attack liberal conformity on sexual, racial, environmental and other voguish issues."

Item: "At the State University at Binghamton," Frank Herron wrote in The Syracuse Herald-Journal in March, "a meeting of a group formed to resist the pressure to conform to 'politically correct' speech was crashed by about 150 students, some carrying sticks."

Distantly related item: "A professor at the University of California at Santa Barbara noted that *pet* had become a derogatory term," wrote Stephanie Schorow of The Associated Press, "at the insistence of animal rights activists. The politically correct term was now *companion animal.*" When the professor facetiously wondered if some magazine centerfold models would soon be called Penthouse *Companion Animals,* 15 women promptly filed sexual harassment charges.

Linguistically sensitive Newsweek warns students: "Watch what you say. There's a politically correct way to talk about race, sex and ideas." The New Republic rejects that discipline, seeing "the imposition of political correctness" as meaning "our universities, which should strive for an identity in contradistinction to the world at large, have become distillations of our bitterest social divisions."

□

The first citation I can find for the incendiary phrase dates from a December 1975 statement by Karen De-Crow, then president of the National Organization for Women. She claimed that a dissident faction felt that feminism was only for "white, middle-class, straight women" and insisted that NOW was moving in the "intellectually and *politically correct* direction." The phrase began as an assertion by liberal (progressive, concerned) activists and then was turned into an attack phrase by conservative (right-wing, heartless) passivists.

The first word in the phrase is a "premodifier" — an adverb that modifies and then fuses with an adjective to form a compound modifying a noun. As Quirk, Greenbaum, Leech and Svartvik note in their "Grammar of Contemporary English," such adverb premodifiers often express viewpoints: *politically expedient, artistically justifiable, economically feasible, theoretically sound, ethically wrong,* and as girls from Brooklyn said of boys from Bronx Science, *geographically undesirable.* Of all these married modifiers, *politically correct* has become the most tightly wedded.

The origin is in *correct thinking.* "Where Do Correct Ideas Come From?" was the title of a 1963 thought by Chairman Mao Zedong, one of those later collected in a little red book that sold in numbers that still make publishers sigh. The chairman thought on: "Do they drop from the skies? No. Are they innate in the mind? No. They come from social practice, and from it alone."

The Maoist phrase was also translated as *correct thinking,* as shown in this 1977 use by Kenneth Turan of The Washington Post on the glories of Dr. Brown's Cel-Ray tonic: "This beverage not only quenches your thirst . . . but serves as a talisman and a cultural rite as well, a sign of goodness and correct thinking that even Chairman Mao would have appreciated."

To dedicated Communists, *correct thinking* was "the disciplined inculcation of a party line expressed in all forms of social and political intercourse." When it was adopted self-mockingly by conservatives in the United States, it meant usually "one of us." The columnist George F. Will described Irena Kirkland in 1985 as "a life-affirming person and one of Washington's dozen or so Correct Thinkers."

To both left and right, then, *correct* came to mean "reflecting the opinions of the group"; in the late '80s, when the right went after the conformity of the left on college campuses, the affirmation of *politically correct* became an epithet.

Briefly now to the issue of vocabulary vigilantes who try to enforce "correct" language. Examples of taboo-boos can be found in the list compiled by fellows at the University of Missouri Multicultural Management Program: *feminine* "can be objectionable to some women"; *codger* or *geezer,* "an objectionable reference to a senior citizen"; Jew, "some people find use of *Jew* alone offensive and prefer *Jewish person*"; and *swarthy,* "avoid all unnecessary references to skin color, such as yellow."

A Syracuse law student, Dennis F. Chiappetta Jr., notes in a recent letter about all such lingo-policing: "From what I can see, the end they seek is the removal of all language that brings to anyone's mind a negative or in any form degrading image. Is this possible? Can any language be written so 'correctly' as to invoke only pleasant or neutral feelings?"

My correspondent, a profound rather than correct thinker, follows up: "With the removal of terms of derision, will the prejudices also disappear — or will these new terms adopt connotations that users of the old terms may have seen in those terms?"

The opinions of Lex Irregs are solicited; we'll limit the debate here to specific choices of words rather than diatribes about "correct" subjects and attitudes.

Some words of derision hurt; they should be identified as slurs in at least one sense and avoided. Others — from *pert* and *petite* to *soulful* and *wannabe* — are getting a bad rap from the hypersensitive. The communication question to be asked is not "Could this possibly offend?" but "Does this get the intended point across?"

New York Times Service

lighted quote). What attitudes would you say are conveyed by these features?
5. In paragraph 3, the writer makes use of alliteration. How does it contribute to the tone of the paragraph?
6. Most journalists strive toward an objectivity which is more or less intentional, more or less sincere. Can you see any evidence in the article of a striving for impartiality?

William Safire: "'Correct Thinking' on the Campus"

What does "PC" stand for? If your impulse is to blurt out "personal computer," you have gone software in the head. If those letters evoke memories of the Peace Corps, you are antediluvian. A percentage of postcards from hypochondriacs will insist that the initials stands for the Latin direction *post cibum,* "after meals," the only digestively conducive time to pop certain pills.

Those of us with slanguistic *Fingerspitzengefühl,* however, know that the initials stand for the most controversial phrase on college campuses today: *politically correct.* In "Thatch," a comic strip by Jeff Shesol of Brown University, a heroic character slips on a cape and supermanly tights with "PC" emblazoned on his chest. It's not a nerd, it's not a plane, it's ... Politically Correct Person!

"There is a new McCarthyism that has spread over American college campuses," writes Max Lerner, an old-line liberal. "We call it 'political correctness.'" The new Random House Webster's College Dictionary defines the term as "marked by or adhering to a typically progressive orthodoxy on issues involving especially race, gender, sexual affinity or ecology."

I would edit that definition to denote *politically correct* as "an adverbially premodified adjectival lexical unit used to attack liberal conformity on sexual, racial, environmental and other voguish issues."

Item: "At the State University of Binghamton," Frank Herron wrote in The Syracuse Herald-Journal in March, "a meeting of a group formed to resist the pressure to conform to 'politically correct' speech was crashed by about 150 students, some carrying sticks."

Distantly related item: "A professor at the University of California at Santa Barbara noted that *pet* had become a derogatory term," wrote Stephanie Schorow of The Associated Press, "at the insistence of animal rights activists. The politically correct term was now *companion animal.*" When the professor facetiously wondered if some magazine centerfold models would soon be called Penthouse *Companion Animals,* 15 women promptly filed sexual harassment charges.

Linguistically sensitive Newsweek warns students: "Watch what you say. There's a politically correct way to talk about race, sex and ideas." The New Republic rejects that discipline, seeing "the imposition of political correctness" as meaning "our universities, which should strive for an identity in contradistinction to the world at large, have become distillations of our bitterest social divisions."

The first citation I can find for the incendiary phrase dates from a December 1975 statement by Karen DeCrow, then president of the National Organization for Women. She claimed that a dissident faction felt that feminism was only for "white, middle-class, straight women" and insisted NOW was moving in the "intellectually and *politically correct* direction." The phrase began as an assertion by liberal (progressive, concerned) activists and then was turned into an attack phrase by conservative (right-wing, heartless) passivists.

The first word in the phrase is a "premodifier" – an adverb that modifies and then fuses with an adjective to form a compound modifying a noun. As Quirk, Greenbaum, Leech and Svartvik note in their "Grammar of Contemporary English," such adverb premodifiers often express viewpoints: *politically expedient, artistically justifiable, economically feasible, theoretically sound, ethically wrong,* and as girls from Brooklyn said of boys from Bronx Science, *geographically undesirable.* Of all these married modifiers, *politically correct* has become the most tightly wedded.

The origin is in *correct thinking.* "Where Do Correct Ideas Come From?" was the title of a 1963 thought by Chairman Mao Zedong, one of those later collected in a little red book that sold in numbers that still make publishers sigh. The chairman thought on: "Do they drop from the skies? No. Are they innate in the mind? No. They come from social practice, and from it alone."

The Maoist phrase was also translated as *correct thinking,* as shown in this 1977 use by Kenneth Turan of The Washington Post on the glories of Dr. Brown's Cel-Ray tonic: "This beverage not only quenches your thirst ... but serves as a talisman and a cultural rite as well, a sign of goodness and correct thinking that even Chairman Mao would have appreciated."

To dedicated Communists, *correct thinking* was "the disciplined inculcation of a party line expressed in all forms of social and political intercourse." When it was adopted self-mockingly by conservatives in the United States, it meant usually "one of us." The columnist George F. Will described Irena Kirkland in 1985 as "a life-affirming person and one of Washington's dozen or so Correct Thinkers."

To both left and right, then, *correct* came to mean "reflecting the opinions of the group"; in the late '80s, when the right went after the conformity of the left on college campuses, the affirmation of *politically correct* became an epithet.

Briefly now to the issue of vocabulary vigilantes who try to enforce "correct" language. Examples of taboo-boos can be found in the list compiled by fellows at the University of Missouri Multicultural Management Program: *feminine* "can be objectionable to some women"; *codger* or *geezer,* "an objectionable reference to a senior citizen"; Jew, "some people find use of *Jew* alone offensive and prefer *Jewish person*"; and *swarthy,* "avoid all unnecessary references to skin color, such as yellow."

A Syracuse law student, Dennis F. Chiappetta Jr., notes in a recent letter about all such lingo-policing: "From what I can see, the end they seek is the removal of all language that brings to anyone's mind a negative or in any form degrading image. Is this possible? Can any language be written so 'correctly' as to invoke only pleasant or neutral feelings?"

My correspondent, a profound rather than correct thinker, follows up: "With the removal of terms of derision, will the prejudices also disappear – or will these new terms adopt connotations that users of the old terms may have seen in those terms?"

The opinions of Lex Irregs are solicited; we'll limit the debate here to specific choices of words rather than diatribes about "correct" subjects and attitudes.

Some words of derision hurt; they should be identified as slurs in at least one sense and avoided. Others – from *pert* and *petite* to *soulful* and *wannabe* – are getting a bad rap from the hypersensitive. The communication question to be asked is not "Could this possibly offend?" but "Does this get the intended point across?"

© New York Times 1991.

Exercise 3

After having read "'Correct Thinking' on the Campus," consider the following:

1. What is your general impression of this headline as compared with "Thought Police"? Comment on the effect of placing 'Correct Thinking' within quotation marks. Those who are

familiar with William Safire's column know that it regularly
deals with language use. But even for those who do not know
this, what is communicated by classifying the article under
Language?

2. Considering only the first two paragraphs, how would you characterize their tone? What, for example, is the effect of directly
addressing readers as "you"? What other features would you
pick out as responsible for establishing the tone?

3. As in "Thought Police," it would have been possible for Safire
to start the article somewhat later, in paragraph 3. Why do you
think he chose to start his topic in the way he did?

4. The rest of the article's first section introduces a number of
quotations from various sources. Consider each one in terms of
its degree of authority and the attitude it is designed to pro-
mote. Comment on the effect of the order of the two quotations
in the final paragraph of the section.

5. In which portions of the text does Safire establish his credentials as a scholar? In what way do these credentials contribute
to his persuasiveness?

6. Pick out any examples of alliteration that you find particularly
striking. How would you characterize its effect in these instances?

7. Comparing once more with "Thought Police," where in the
article do you see evidence of the journalist's striving for objectivity?

8. How, finally, would you characterize Safire's position on political correctness?

"Political correctness" is a concept that has been used throughout
our century, but it has gained new currency in the 1980s and
1990s as disadvantaged groups, particularly in the United States,
have challenged the prejudices and the cultural hegemony of the
dominant classes. At the beginning of this period the term had a
positive ring to it; to be "politically correct" was to be non-racist,
non-sexist, etc. Later it took on the negative associations of a
repressive moralism which in its extreme form turned into a fanat-
ical hunt for scapegoats among the "politically incorrect."

As you have seen, the above exercises raise the issue of objectivity in writing. Contemporary critical theory questions the notion of objective (re)presentation and argues that all statements – even empirical ones – are grounded in and reveal the speaker's set of beliefs and values. Writers' attitudes toward their subject are inevitably conveyed in the selection and ordering of the material they present. Selection takes place at all levels, ranging from decisions about which facts and arguments to include, to choices of words and syntactic patterns. In many cases it will also involve the use of devices that have traditionally been associated with literature, such as plot, figures of speech, and alliteration.

Although we have chosen to deal with newspaper and magazine texts in this unit, the principles we draw attention to apply to many types of texts. In Unit Three we continue our discussion of these principles in the blend of narrative and expository prose that characterizes history writing.

WRITTEN ASSIGNMENT

In a newspaper article of your choice, analyze the first few paragraphs in terms of the following features:
- the *selection* of the material: what has been included? left out? emphasized (foregrounded)?
- the *ordering* of the material: what comes first? what comes next? with what effect?
- *word choices*: why has one synonym rather than another been chosen? That is, consider the effect of the words' connotations in the context.
- the use of such literary devices as narrative, metaphors, and alliteration.

See "Rhetoric" in the Glossary.

The rhetoric of reporting and persuasion in history texts

In this unit we continue our analysis of the various ways in which even the most apparently objective texts convey a point of view. We do this by looking at how three historians describe Abraham Lincoln. We also explore the links between history and other types of text.

Material:

> Herbert Agar, excerpt from *The Price of Union* (1950)
> John A. Garraty, excerpt from *The American Nation* (1983)
> Howard Zinn, excerpt from *A People's History of the United States* (1980)

We shall start by asking you to identify your expectations of what a "history" text should be like.

EXERCISE 1

1. Before you read the three texts below, jot down a few notes on what you remember hearing about Abraham Lincoln, drawing upon whatever associations his name evokes in your mind.
2. Similarly, jot down a few notes on what you expect to find in a history text.

Now read the three excerpts and answer the questions that follow.

Note: Although these texts are all excerpts, we shall treat them as units in their own right; that is, we do not take into account the influence of their original contexts on our interpretations.

Herbert Agar: *The Price of Union*

The hard work of farming – and of clearing fresh land, fencing it, building new cabins – turned Lincoln into a physical giant: over six feet four in height and with a strength that became legendary even in the rough West. But he never lost his desire to learn. He would walk miles to borrow a book – and what was far more unusual, having borrowed it, and read it, he would actually think about it. He was one of the very few people who could go on thinking after he had stopped reading or talking. He never learned to turn his back, except briefly, on the great defeating questions of life and death and destiny. This may be why he was unhappy, and why he was great. He was oppressed by the mystery but never frightened; so in his long days alone – as a boy on the frontier or on a river-boat, as a man driving his buggy across the empty prairies from one county courthouse to another – he did not close or distract his mind or his spirit. He continued his rapt, sometimes morbid, search for understanding – and one day (although he never knew it) he became the wisest man in America. A fellow lawyer described Lincoln in court when he was lost in thinking: "He seemed to be pursuing in his mind some specific painful subject, regularly and systematically through various sinuosities; and his sad face would assume, at times, deeper phases of grief. No relief came till he was roused by the adjournment of court, when he emerged from his cage of gloom, like one awakened from sleep."

During such hours of abstraction, which came upon him from the time he was a child, Lincoln was not pursuing a mystic trance: he was trying to think. This is perhaps the most difficult of undertakings, and the rarest. Lincoln's addiction to it may explain why all his life he grew in mercy and in understanding. At forty he was a leading Western lawyer and an unsuccessful Congressman; at fifty he was not only a national figure, but in his own section he was an important moral force; at fifty-six, when he was murdered, he was one of the masters of his age. He was mourned in Europe and Asia by men who knew nothing about him, or about America, except that someone good had gone from the earth. The accidents of politics may make a man world-famous; but only richness of spirit can make him world-respected. In Lincoln the richness came from thought, from his painful prolonged brooding, "wrapped in abstraction and gloom." He had no clear religious faith. He believed in God, but seemingly in an unconsoling God. He said it was his destiny to live in twilight, feeling and reasoning his way through life. He said he was like the man in St. Mark: "Lord, I believe; help Thou mine unbelief."

If Lincoln's "feeling and reasoning" made him wise, pious, and subtle, it also made him irreverent, bawdy, impudent, ribald, and cruelly funny. He was the best storyteller in the West and the best mimic. He found it seductively easy to make an opponent look absurd; but he seldom used this power in court against a witness. He saved it to torment his political foes. His broad and racy laughter was probably his salvation. "Lincoln's humour," wrote Francis Grierson, "was the balance-pole of his genius that enabled him to cross the most giddy heights without losing his head."*

* *The Valley of Shadows,* 1848 ed., p. 196. Grierson's long-ignored classic, consisting of "recollections of scenes and episodes of my early life in Illinois and Missouri," was published in 1909. It gives far the best picture of the Western men to whom Lincoln first became a hero.

From Herbert Agar, *The Price of Union.* Boston: Houghton Mifflin Company, 1950.

John A. Garraty: *The Coming of the Civil War*

After a towering figure has passed from the stage, it is always difficult to discover what he was like before his rise to prominence. This is especially true of Lincoln, who changed greatly when power and responsibility and fame came to him. Lincoln was not unknown in 1858, but his career had not been distinguished. He was born in Kentucky in 1809, and the story of his early life can be condensed, as he once said himself, into a single line from Gray's *Elegy:* "The short and simple annals of the poor." His illiterate, ne'er-do-well father, Thomas Lincoln, was a typical frontier wanderer. When Abraham was 7 the family moved to Indiana. In 1830 they pushed west again into southern Illinois. The boy received almost no formal schooling, but he had a good mind and was extremely ambitious. He cut loose from his family, made a trip to New Orleans, and for a time managed a general store in New Salem, Illinois. When barely 25 he won a seat in the Illinois legislature as a Whig. He studied law and was admitted to the bar in 1836.

Lincoln remained in the legislature until 1842, displaying a perfect willingness to adopt the Whig position on all issues. In 1846 he was elected to Congress. While not engaged in politics he worked at the law, maintaining an office in Springfield and following the circuit, taking a variety of cases, few of much importance. He earned a decent but by no means sumptuous living. After one term in Congress his political career petered out. He seemed fated to pass his remaining years as a typical small-town lawyer.

Even during this period Lincoln's personality was enormously complex. His bawdy sense of humor and his endless fund of stories and tall tales made him a legend first in Illinois and then in Washington. He was admired in Illinois as a powerful and expert axman and a champion wrestler. He was thoroughly at home with toughs like the "Clary's Grove Boys" of New Salem and in the convivial atmosphere of a party caucus. But in a society where most men drank heavily, he never touched liquor. And he was subject to periods of melancholy so profound as to appear almost psychopathic. Friends spoke of him as having "cat fits," and he wrote of himself in the early 1840s: "I am now the most miserable man living. If what I felt were equally distributed to the whole human family, there would not be one cheerful face on earth."

In a region swept by repeated waves of religious revivalism, Lincoln managed to be at once a man of calm spirituality and a skeptic without appearing offensive to conventional believers. He was a party wheelhorse, a corporation lawyer, even a railroad lobbyist, yet his reputation for integrity was stainless.

The revival of the slavery controversy in 1854 stirred Lincoln deeply. No abolitionist, he had always tried to take a "realistic" view of the problem. The Kansas–Nebraska bill led him to see the moral issue more clearly. "If slavery is not wrong, nothing is wrong," he stated with the clarity and simplicity of expression for which he later became famous. Compromises made for the sake of sectional harmony had always sought to preserve as much territory as possible for freedom. Yet unlike most northern Free Soilers, he did not blame the southerners for slavery. "They are just what we would be in their situation," he confessed.

The fairness and moderation of his position combined with its moral force won Lincoln many admirers in the great body of citizens who were trying to reconcile their generally low opinion of blacks and their patriotic desire to avoid an issue that threatened the Union with their growing conviction that slavery was sinful. *Anything* that aided slavery was wrong, Lincoln argued. But before casting the first stone, every northerner should look into his own heart: "If there be a man amongst us who is so impatient of [slavery] as a wrong as to disregard its actual presence among us and the difficulty of getting rid of it suddenly in a satisfactory way ... that man is misplaced if he is on our platform." And Lincoln confessed:

If all earthly power were given to me, I should not know what to do as to the existing institution. But ... [this] furnishes no more excuse for permitting slavery to go into our free territory than it would for reviving the African slave trade.

Thus Lincoln was at once compassionate toward the slaveowner and stern toward the institution. "'A house divided against itself cannot stand,'" he warned. "I believe this government cannot endure permanently half slave and half free." Without minimizing the difficulties or urging a hasty and ill-considered solution, Lincoln demanded that the people look toward a day, however remote, when not only Kansas but the entire country would be free.

Selected excerpt from Chapter 14 from *The American Nation: A History of the United States*, 5th ed., by John A. Garraty. Copyright © 1966, 1971, 1975, 1979, 1983 by John A. Garraty. Reprinted by permission of HarperCollins Publishers, Inc.

Howard Zinn: *A People's History of the United States*

John Brown was executed by the state of Virginia with the approval of the national government. It was the national government which, while weakly enforcing the law ending the slave trade, sternly enforced the laws providing for the return of fugitives to slavery. It was the national government that, in Andrew Jackson's administration, collaborated with the South to keep abolitionist literature out of the mails in the southern states. It was the Supreme Court of the United States that declared in 1857 that the slave Dred Scott could not sue for his freedom because he was not a person, but property.

Such a national government would never accept an end to slavery by rebellion. It would end slavery only under conditions controlled by whites, and only when required by the political and economic needs of the business elite of the North. It was Abraham Lincoln who combined perfectly the needs of business, the political ambition of the new Republican party, and the rhetoric of humanitarianism. He would keep the abolition of slavery not at the top of his list of priorities, but close enough to the top so it could be pushed there temporarily by abolitionist pressures and by practical political advantage.

Lincoln could skillfully blend the interests of the very rich and the interests of the black at a moment in history when these interests met. And he could link these two with a growing section of Americans, the white, up-and-coming, economically ambitious, politically active middle class. As Richard Hofstadter puts it:

Thoroughly middle class in his ideas, he spoke for those millions of Americans who had begun their lives as hired workers – as farm hands, clerks, teachers, mechanics, flatboat men, and rail-splitters – and had passed into the ranks of landed farmers, prosperous grocers, lawyers, merchants, physicians and politicians.

Lincoln could argue with lucidity and passion against slavery on moral grounds, while acting cautiously in practical politics. He believed "that the institution of slavery is founded on injustice and bad policy, but that the promulgation of abolition doctrines tends to increase rather than abate its evils." (Put against this Frederick Douglass's statement on struggle, or Garrison's "Sir, slavery will not be overthrown without excitement, a most tremendous excitement.") Lincoln read the Constitution strictly, to mean that Congress, because of the Tenth Amendment (reserving to the states powers not specifically given to the national government), could not constitutionally bar slavery in the states.

When it was proposed to abolish slavery in the District of Columbia, which did not have the rights of a state but was directly under the jurisdiction of Congress, Lincoln said this would be Constitutional, but it should not be done unless the people in the District wanted it. Since most there were white, this killed the idea. As Hofstadter said of Lincoln's statement, it "breathes the fire of an uncompromising insistence on moderation."

Lincoln refused to denounce the Fugitive Slave Law publicly. He wrote to a friend: "I confess I hate to see the poor creatures hunted down ... but I bite my lips and keep quiet." And when he did propose, in 1849, as a Congressman, a resolution to abolish slavery in the District of Columbia, he accompanied this with a section requiring local authorities to arrest and return fugitive slaves coming into Washington. (This led Wendell Phillips, the Boston abolitionist, to refer to him years later as "that slavehound from Illinois.") He opposed slavery, but could not see blacks as equals, so a constant theme in his approach was to free the slaves and to send them back to Africa.

In his 1858 campaign in Illinois for the Senate against Stephen Douglas, Lincoln spoke differently depending on the views of his listeners (and also perhaps depending on how close it was to the election). Speaking in northern Illinois in July (in Chicago), he said:

Let us discard all this quibbling about this man and the other man, this race and that race and the other race being inferior, and therefore they must be placed in an inferior position. Let us discard all these things, and unite as one people throughout this land, until we shall once more stand up declaring that all men are created equal.

Two months later in Charleston, in southern Illinois, Lincoln told his audience:

> I will say, then, that I am not, nor ever have been, in favor of bringing about in any way the social and political equality of the white and black races (applause); that I am not, nor ever have been, in favor of making voters or jurors of negroes, nor of qualifying them to hold office, nor to intermarry with white people....

And inasmuch as they cannot so live, while they do remain together there must be the position of superior and inferior, and I as much as any other man am in favor of having the superior position assigned to the white race.

From Howard Zinn, *A People's History of the United States*. London: Longman, 1980. Reprinted by permission from Balkin Agency, Inc.

EXERCISE 2

1. Which of the texts is closest to your own portrait of Lincoln? If any of the portraits surprised you, explain why.
2. Which text best confirms your idea of a historical account?

Go back now to the texts and answer the following questions in note form in preparation for class discussion:

EXERCISE 3

1. What kind of man would you say emerges from each portrayal of Lincoln?
2. What title would you suggest for each piece? Explain your choice of titles by referring to features in the texts which seem to you to justify your choice.

We will now take a look at the texts in some detail.

EXERCISE 4

Working on each text separately, do the following:
1. Underline the facts given in each text.
2. Underline (in a different color, for example) what you consider to be the key terms used to describe Lincoln.
3. Check the texts for their use of quotations. From what sources do the quotations come?
4. Look at the ratio between facts and quotations in each text. Do you see any differences between them in this respect?

EXERCISE 5

1. In Agar's and Garraty's texts, try to identify the little stories or mini-narrative(s) about Lincoln that the first paragraphs offer. In what genres would you expect to find these "plot" elements? What theme(s) would you say they contribute to?
2. In what way is the opening paragraph of Zinn's text different from the other two texts? What "story" does it tell? What do you think is its point?
3. What other "stories" about Lincoln can you identify in the excerpts? What assessments of Lincoln do they lead to?

EXERCISE 6

1. Underline the portions of Agar's text that you think could be omitted without changing its information content. What, then, would you say is the role of these phrases and sentences in the text?
2. In Zinn's text, what is the effect of the repeated use of the marked syntactic pattern "It was the ..." at the beginning of sentences 2–4? Look also at the construction of the sentences in paragraphs 4 and 6. Several of them set up oppositions by using words like *while* and *but*. What kind of information is presented in the first half of each sentence? What kind in the second? What is the effect of distributing the information in the sentences in this way?

EXERCISE 7

Compare the last paragraphs of the three texts in terms of the following questions:

1. What impression of Lincoln does each paragraph leave us with?
2. What is the effect of ending the texts with these impressions?

Finally, answer the following questions and conclude by evaluating the three passages:

EXERCISE 8

1. How is the presence of the authors signaled in the three texts?
2. How would you characterize each author's attitude toward Lincoln?
3. Classify the texts in terms of the relative "subjectivity" and "objectivity" of their accounts of Lincoln. Support your classification with textual evidence.
4. Which of the portraits do you find most persuasive? Why? (Please compare your answer to this question with you answers to the questions in Exercise 2.)

As you have seen while doing these exercises, all three texts are the result of choices made by their authors. They have decided how to start and how to end their pieces; they have decided what facts about Lincoln to include or to exclude; and they have told varying stories about Lincoln. They have also chosen to use a certain kind of vocabulary (e.g. *brooding* rather than *reflecting* in the middle of the second paragraph of Agar's text). All of these choices combine to convey a certain point of view on Lincoln.

Roland Barthes has used the term "personal thematics" to refer to the persuasive effect of such choices in history texts. He argues that historians appear to absent themselves from their texts so that history "seems to tell itself." In this way they create what he calls a "referential illusion" (1986, pp. 132–33). In fact, Barthes writes, if historians did not explain and hence give meaning to the facts and events they report, there would be nothing left but a "void of pure series" (pp. 137–38). Inevitably, then, the author's "personal thematics" imposes structure on his/her material (e.g. by developing the theme of a historical personage's fame, or of the rise and fall of a civilization). Barthes concludes that the historian "collects not so much facts as signifiers" and that "the real is never anything but a meaning" (p. 138).

WRITTEN ASSIGNMENTS

1. As the culmination of the thinking you have done in the above exercises, write a comparison of the three portrayals of Lincoln in terms of the following features:
   - the selection of material: which "facts" have been included, which excluded?
   - the ordering of material: with what material have the writers chosen to start their pieces? Do they follow a chronological order, or some other order? How do they end their texts? What is conveyed by such choices?
   - the inclusion of story elements and the points made by the use of mini-narratives.
   - the choice of words and syntactic structures.
2. Analyze one or more encyclopedia entries on Abraham Lincoln with reference to the issue of objectivity and subjectivity in history writing.

See "History" in the Glossary.

Unit Four

Literature and "reality": the role of genre expectations

In this unit we look at some of the expectations with which we read texts. Many of these expectations are grounded in the way we decipher the signs of well-established conventions. We acquire these conventions in the process of growing up in a given culture (or as we are exposed to the culture of a new language), that is, in the process of acculturation.

We start by looking at the way genre establishes a "horizon of expectations" for readers. We then go on to address some questions raised by the convention of verisimilitude; that is, we discuss the tensions that often arise between literal ("obvious") readings and metaphorical or less "obvious" ones set off by various "oddities" in the text.

Material:

> Katherine Mansfield, "A Suburban Fairy Tale" (1917)
> William Carlos Williams, "This Is Just to Say" (1934)
> Sylvia Plath, "Mushrooms" (1960)

Section One

Read the story below *before* looking at any of the exercise material.

Katherine Mansfield: "A Suburban Fairy Tale"

Mr. and Mrs. B. sat at breakfast in the cosy red dining-room of their "snug little crib just under half-an-hour's run from the City."

There was a good fire in the grate – for the dining-room was the living-room as well – the two windows overlooking the cold empty garden patch were closed, and the air smelled agreeably of bacon and eggs, toast and coffee. Now that this rationing business was really over Mr. B. made a point of a thoroughly good tuck-in before facing the very real perils of the day. He didn't mind who knew it – he was a true Englishman about his breakfast – he had to have it; he'd cave in without it, and if you told him that these Continental chaps could get through half the morning's work he did on a roll and a cup of coffee – you simply didn't know what you were talking about.

Mr. B. was a stout youngish man who hadn't been able – worse luck – to chuck his job and join the Army; he'd tried for four years to get another chap to take his place, but it was no go. He sat at the head of the table reading the *Daily Mail.* Mrs. B. was a youngish plump little body, rather like a pigeon. She sat opposite, preening herself behind the coffee set and keeping an eye of warning love on little B. who perched between them, swathed in a napkin and tapping the top of a soft-boiled egg.

Alas! Little B. was not at all the child that such parents had every right to expect. He was no fat little trot, no dumpling, no firm little pudding. He was undersized for his age, with legs like macaroni, tiny claws, soft, soft hair that felt like mouse fur and big wide-open eyes. For some strange reason everything in life seemed the wrong size for Little B. – too big and too violent. Everything knocked him over, took the wind out of his feeble sails and left him gasping and frightened. Mr. and Mrs. B. were quite powerless to prevent this; they could only pick him up after the mischief was done – and try to set him going again. And Mrs. B. loved him as only weak children are loved – and when Mr. B. thought what a marvellous little chap he was too – thought of the spunk of the little man, he – well he – by George – he ...

"Why aren't there two kinds of eggs?" said Little B. "Why aren't there little eggs for children and big eggs like what this one is for grown-ups?"

"Scotch hares," said Mr. B. "Fine Scotch hares for 5s. 3d. How about getting one, old girl?"

"It would be a nice change, wouldn't it?" said Mrs. B. "Jugged."

And they looked across at each other and there floated between them the Scotch hare in its rich gravy with stuffing balls and a white pot of red-current jelly accompanying it.

"We might have had it for the week-end," said Mrs. B. "But the butcher has promised me a nice little sirloin and it seems a pity" ... Yes, it did, and yet" ... Dear me, it was very difficult to decide. The hare would have been such a change – on the other hand, could you beat a really nice little sirloin?"

"There's hare soup, too," said Mr. B., drumming his fingers on the table. "Best soup in the world!"

"O-oh!" cried Little B. so suddenly and sharply that it gave them quite a start – "Look at the whole lot of sparrows flown on to our lawn" – he waved his spoon. "Look at them," he cried. "Look!" And while he spoke, even though the windows were closed, they heard a loud shrill cheeping and chirping from the garden.

"Get on with your breakfast like a good boy, do," said his mother, and his father said, "You stick to the egg, old man, and look sharp about it."

"But look at them – look at them all hopping," he cried. "They don't keep still not for a minute. Do you think they're hungry, father?"

Cheek-a-cheep-cheep-cheek! cried the sparrows.

"Best postpone it perhaps till next week," said Mr. B., "and trust to luck they're still to be had then."

"Yes, perhaps that would be wiser," said Mrs. B.

Mr. B. picked another plum out of his paper.

"Have you bought any of those controlled dates yet?"

"I managed to get two pounds yesterday," said Mrs. B.

"Well, a date pudding's a good thing," said Mr. B. And they looked across at each other and there floated between them a dark round pudding covered with creamy sauce. "It would be a nice change, wouldn't it?" said Mrs. B.

Outside on the grey frozen grass the funny eager sparrows hopped and fluttered. They were never for a moment still. They cried, flapped their ungainly wings. Little B., his egg finished, got down, took his bread and marmalade to eat at the window.

"Do let us give them some crumbs," he said. "Do open the window, father, and throw them something. Father, *please!*"

"Oh, don't nag, child," said Mrs. B., and his father said – "Can't go opening windows, old man. You'd get your head bitten off."

"But they're hungry," cried Little B., and the sparrows' little voices were like ringing of little knives being sharpened. *Cheek-a-cheep-cheep-cheek!* they cried.

Little B. dropped his bread and marmalade inside the china flower-pot in front of the window. He slipped behind the thick curtains to see better, and

Mr. and Mrs. B. went on reading about what you could get now without coupons – no more ration books after May – a glut of cheese – a glut of it – whole cheeses revolved in the air between them like celestial bodies.

Suddenly as Little B. watched the sparrows on the grey frozen grass, they grew, they changed, still flapping and squeaking. They turned into tiny little boys, in brown coats, dancing, jigging outside, up and down outside the window squeaking, "Want something to eat, want something to eat!" Little B. held with both hands to the curtain. "Father," he whispered, "Father! They're not sparrows. They're little boys. Listen, Father!" But Mr. and Mrs. B. would not hear. He tried again. "Mother," he whispered. "Look at the little boys. They're not sparrows, Mother!" But nobody noticed his nonsense.

"All this talk about famine," cried Mr. B., "all a Fake, all a Blind."

With white shining faces, their arms flapping in the big coats, the little boys danced. "Want something to eat, want something to eat."

"Father," muttered Little B. "Listen, Father! Mother, listen, please!"

"Really!" said Mrs. B. "The noise those birds are making! I've never heard such a thing."

"Fetch me my shoes, old man," said Mr. B.

Cheek-a-cheep-cheep-cheek! said the sparrows.

Now where had that child got to? "Come and finish your nice cocoa, my pet," said Mrs. B.

Mr. B. lifted the heavy cloth and whispered, "Come on, Rover," but no little dog was there.

"He's behind the curtain," said Mrs. B.

"He never went out of the room," said Mr. B.

Mrs. B. went over to the window and Mr. B. followed. And they looked out. There on the grey frozen grass, with a white, white face, the little boy's thin arms flapping like wings, in front of them all, the smallest, tiniest was Little B. Mr. and Mrs. B. heard his voice above all the voices. "Want something to eat, want something to eat."

Somehow, somehow, they opened the window. "You shall! All of you. Come in *at once*. Old man! Little man!"

But it was too late. The little boys were changed into sparrows again, and away they flew – out of sight – out of call.

(1917)

EXERCISE 1

1. Read through the story again, marking anything that struck you in any way – words, phrases, passages that pleased, interested, or puzzled you. It might be a detail, an episode, a character, a name, a series of repetitions, or some other feature.
2. Go back and look at your marked words/passages and write down questions or comments about them.
3. Discuss your chosen passages and your questions and comments in groups of two or three.

The questions in Exercise 2 refer you to one of the basic presuppositions of literary criticism, namely that associations are an important part of the construction of meaning in literary texts (and, indeed, in many other types of texts). So let us look at some of the details in the story.

EXERCISE 2

1. As you may have observed, there are a number of animal images in the story. Mrs. B., for example, is compared to a pigeon. The story's central incident is a transformation of sparrows into boys and then back to birds. Why do you think Mansfield has chosen to make the birds sparrows rather than, say, geese or, again, pigeons?
2. The sparrows are described as turning into "tiny little boys, in brown coats." Sparrows *are* brown, so this could just be a literal description, but can you think of any associations that "brown coats" might have that extend beyond the sparrows to the social reality evoked by the story?
3. In Little B.'s first appeal to his parents to take notice of the sparrows, he urges, "Do let us give them some crumbs." If we altered the sentence to, for instance, "Do let us feed them," the associations of *crumbs* would be lost. What might some of these associations be?

From the point of view of everyday reality, and hence within the convention of realism, it is impossible for little boys to turn into sparrows and fly away. The climax of the story thus involves us in a world of magic transformations. And yet the story also makes many references to a recognizable social reality. Let us consider how Mansfield combines the magical with the realistic in the story. We shall begin with the realistic elements.

EXERCISE 3

1. Note that the editor has provided a date in parentheses at the end of the text. What important historical events does 1917 bring to mind? Do any of them seem relevant to the story?
2. Go through the text and mark all the features that you feel belong to the area of social or historical reality.

We shall now turn to the fairy tale elements.

EXERCISE 4

1. Make a quick list of the settings and characters you usually associate with fairy tales.
2. A typical pattern in fairy tales is the use of three (three brothers, three wishes, three tests, etc.). What patterns of three are there in the story? Are they related to a fairy tale world or to English society (or perhaps to both at the same time)?
3. Go through the story and mark any other features that you feel belong to the fairy tale genre.

You will notice that the title of Mansfield's story combines two concepts that we usually do not associate together: *suburban* and *fairy tale*. As we go about making sense of the story, we are invited to reconcile the expectations set in motion by the title. Titles often function as signals of genre. For instance, the title of Henry James's *The Portrait of a Lady* evokes the convention of a psychological and/or social verisimilitude. However, it is unusual, as in the case of "A Suburban Fairy Tale," for the genre to be actually named in the title. The title invites the reader to work out some kind of "fit" between the worlds of magic and social reality. In other words, we try to work out an interpretation that will combine both the realistic and the fairy tale elements of the story. This does not mean that the fit will be unproblematic and seamless. The combination may also involve tensions and incompatibilities. (For example, how compatible is the ending of Mansfield's story with what you see as being the typical ending of a fairy tale?)

Many fairy tales imply a moral. For example, in the Disney version of *The Beauty and the Beast*, the beast is turned into a human (a prince) when he has learned how to love. Similarly, in "A Suburban Fairy Tale" the magic transformation in its combination with the historically and socially specific references invites us to read it as a story with a moral, for instance as a parable. The details of family life and the references to war-time conditions (the "realist" genre) in combination with the magic change from animal to human (the fairy tale genre) thus steer our interpretation in the direction of a social parable. The social parable in itself may include several levels; some readers, for instance, emphasize the drama going on in the family, while others see primarily the dramatization of a class conflict.

Section Two

Note: It is important that you do Exercise 1 before you take a look at the next text.

EXERCISE 1

Read the following text and make a note of your reaction to it:

I have eaten the plums that were in the icebox and which you were probably saving for breakfast Forgive me they were delicious so sweet and so cold

What situation would you say is implied in the text? What kind of speaker and addressee could you imagine for it? In what context would you expect to find a text like this? Is there anything in it that surprises you? What is your reaction to the text?

Exercise 2

1. Read the following text and make a note of your reaction to it.

William Carlos Williams: "This Is Just to Say"

This Is Just to Say

I have eaten
the plums
that were in
the icebox

and which
you were probably
saving
for breakfast

Forgive me
they were delicious
so sweet
and so cold
              1934

2. What situation would you say is implied in the text? What kind of speaker and addressee could you imagine for it? In what context would you expect to find a text like this? Is there anything in it that surprises you? What is your reaction to the text?

3. Compare your answers regarding the two texts and make a note of any differences in your interpretations of or responses to them. How would you account for the differences, if any?

4. For what reasons would the second version of the text be called more "literary"?

You will notice how a change in the typographical arrangement of the lines can cause us to change our way of reading a text. This is because the "poetry" arrangement brings into play a cluster of interpretive conventions. We will return to these conventions in the discussion of the next poem.

Section Three

Read the following poem and make a note of your reaction to it.

Sylvia Plath: "Mushrooms"

Overnight, very
Whitely, discreetly,
Very quietly

Our toes, our noses
Take hold on the loam,
Acquire the air.

Nobody sees us,
Stops us, betrays us;
The small grains make room.

Soft fists insist on
Heaving the needles,
The leafy bedding,

Even the paving.
Our hammers, our rams,
Earless and eyeless,

Perfectly voiceless,
Widen the crannies,
Shoulder through holes. We

Diet on water,
On crumbs of shadow,
Bland-mannered, asking

Little or nothing.
So many of us!
So many of us!

We are shelves, we are
Tables, we are meek,
We are edible,

Nudgers and shovers
In spite of ourselves.
Our kind multiplies:

We shall by morning
Inherit the earth.
Our foot's in the door.
1960

EXERCISE 1

1. Now reread the text and make sure you understand all the words. Make a note of any textual items that you find odd. How would you describe the tone and mood of the poem?
2. Write down your first quick interpretation of the poem, supporting it with quotations from the text.
3. Reread the text once again, this time checking whether your interpretation explains all the lines in the poem. Mark any words, phrases, images, or stanzas which you feel baffled by, or which do not quite fit your interpretation.

EXERCISE 2

1. Draw a picture (mental or on paper) of the "world" of the poem, answering the following questions: what is happening? when is it happening? where? in what manner? who are the agents? what are their "attributes"?
2. You may already have noticed a number of oppositions or tensions in the poem, such as that implied in the phrase "soft fists." Are there any other oppositions on the phrase level or in the composition, or in the general meanings generated by the poem? Take a look at the poem's stanzaic and sentence structure. Compare the effect when you read the text disregarding the punctuation marks (that is, when you follow only the stanzaic division) and when you read the text paying attention to the commas, periods, and other punctuation marks.
3. What links do you see between the last stanza and the rest of the poem?
4. What is the relationship between the title and the rest of the poem? How would you approach the poem if there had not been a title at all? Reread the text and suggest a title that you feel would best signal the poem's "meaning."

5. Using the observations you have made, suggest what you would consider the best interpretation of the poem. Is your second interpretation different from your first? Which one helps you explain more of the textual phenomena that you have observed? Are there any troubling moments in the text that none of the readings you have arrived at can explain? How do you react when your own or someone else's interpretation cannot explain all the elements in the text?

To identify a text as "belonging" to a certain genre is to set in motion a set of assumptions about how this text should be read. The process of identifying the text's genre is very complex. Sometimes it is the context in which the text is encountered that signals the genre (a daily newspaper or a *Norton Anthology of English Literature*); sometimes it is the opening lines, as in fairy tales (the "once upon a time" formula), or a "typical" character of a detective in detective fiction; sometimes it is the typography or the length of the text.

One of the most powerful assumptions in reading poetry is that the referential (literal or dictionary) meaning of signs is secondary to their metaphorical meaning, that is, a meaning which is established in the complex coding of the poem. Thus, a *literal* reading of Sylvia Plath's poem would hinge on treating the title as a reference to a species of fungus. In a *metaphorical* reading, "mushrooms" would stand for something else. Yet even the literal reading would be dependent on a poetic convention in which "mushrooms" can speak.

WRITTEN ASSIGNMENTS

1. Write an essay summarizing the points you have reflected upon while working through Exercises 1–4 in the Katherine Mansfield section. A suggested title for the essay would be "The Realistic versus the Fairy Tale: The Effect of Genre Expectations on My Interpretations of 'A Suburban Fairy Tale.'"
2. Write an essay on "Mushrooms" with the title "Literal versus Metaphorical Readings of 'Mushrooms.'"

3. Choose a text you know well and analyze the function of its title in relation to the text's genre conventions.

See "Genre" and "Realism" in the Glossary.

Unit Five

The representation and the reading of gender and race

In this unit we address the issues of gender and race in textual represen-
tation and in the interpretation of texts. We start by discussing how
cultural assumptions about men and women and whites, and non-
whites, function in three literary texts. We then go on to discuss what
is involved in reading texts from gender- and ethnic-specific positions.
Finally, we briefly consider the relation of the literary canon to the lit-
eratures of the groups which have historically occupied a subordinate
position in Western society.

Material:

Section One
William Faulkner, "A Rose for Emily" (1930)
Cleanth Brooks and Robert Penn Warren, excerpt from *Under-*
standing Fiction (1943)
Robert Crosman, excerpt from "How Readers Make Meaning"
(1982)
Judith Fetterley, excerpts from *The Resisting Reader* (1978)

Section Two
Herman Melville, excerpts from "Benito Cereno" (1856)
Toni Morrison, excerpt from *Sula* (1973)

Section One

Read the story below before looking at the exercises.

William Faulkner: "A Rose for Emily"

I

When Miss Emily Grierson died, our whole town went to her funeral: the men through a sort of respectful affection for a fallen monument, the women mostly out of curiosity to see the inside of her house, which no one save an old manservant – a combined gardener and cook – had seen in at least ten years.

It was a big, squarish frame house that had once been white, decorated with cupolas and spires and scrolled balconies in the heavily lightsome style of the seventies, set on what had once been our most select street. But garages and cotton gins had encroached and obliterated even the august names of that neighborhood; only Miss Emily's house was left, lifting its stubborn and coquettish decay above the cotton wagons and the gasoline pumps – an eyesore among eyesores. And now Miss Emily had gone to join the representatives of those august names where they lay in the cedar-bemused cemetery among the ranked and anonymous graves of Union and Confederate soldiers who fell at the battle of Jefferson.

Alive, Miss Emily had been a tradition, a duty and a care; a sort of hereditary obligation upon the town, dating from that day in 1894 when Colonel Sartoris, the mayor – he who fathered the edict that no Negro woman should appear on the streets without an apron – remitted her taxes, the dispensation dating from the death of her father on into perpetuity. Not that Miss Emily would have accepted charity. Colonel Sartoris invented an involved tale to the effect that Miss Emily's father had loaned money to the town, which the town, as a matter of business, preferred this way of repaying. Only a man of Colonel Sartoris' generation and thought could have invented it, and only a woman could have believed it.

When the next generation, with its more modern ideas, became mayors and aldermen, this arrangement created some little dissatisfaction. On the first of the year they mailed her a tax notice. February came, and there was no reply. They wrote her a formal letter, asking her to call at the sheriff's office at her convenience. A week later the mayor wrote her himself, offering to call or send his car for her and received in reply a note on paper of an archaic shape, in a thin flowing calligraphy in faded ink, to the effect that she no longer went out at all. The tax notice was also enclosed, without comment.

They called a special meeting of the Board of Aldermen. A deputation waited upon her, knocked at the door through which no visitor had passed since she ceased giving china-painting lessons eight or ten years earlier. They were admitted by the old Negro into a dim hall from which a stairway mounted into still more shadow. It smelled of dust and disuse – a close, dank smell. The Negro led them into the parlor. It was furnished in heavy, leather-covered furniture. When the Negro opened the blinds of one window, they could see that the leather was cracked; and when they sat down, a faint dust rose sluggishly about their thighs, spinning with slow motes in the single sunray. On a tarnished gilt easel before the fireplace stood a crayon portrait of Miss Emily's father.

They rose when she entered – a small, fat woman in black, with a thin gold chain descending to her waist and vanishing into her belt, leaning on an ebony cane with a tarnished gold head. Her skeleton was small and spare; perhaps that was why what would have been merely plumpness in another was obesity in her. She looked bloated, like a body long submerged in motionless water, and of that pallid hue. Her eyes, lost in the fatty ridges of her face, looked like two small pieces of coal pressed into a lump of dough as they moved from one face to another while the visitors stated their errand.

She did nok ask them to sit. She just stood in the door and listened quietly until the spokesman came to a stumbling halt. Then they could here the invisible watch ticking at the end of the gold chain.

Her voice was dry and cold. "I have no taxes in Jefferson. Colonel Sartoris explained it to me. Perhaps one of you can gain access to the city records and satisfy yourselves."

"But we have. We are the city authorities, Miss Emily. Didn't you get a notice from the sheriff, signed by him?"

"I received a paper, yes," Miss Emily said. "Perhaps he considers himself the sheriff ... I have no taxes in Jefferson."

"But there is nothing on the books to show that, you see. We must go by the –"

"See Colonel Sartoris. I have no taxes in Jefferson."

"But, Miss Emily –"

"See Colonel Sartoris." (Colonel Sartoris had been dead almost ten years.) "I have no taxes in Jefferson. Tobe!" The Negro appeared. "Show these gentlemen out."

II

So she vanquished them, horse and foot, just as she had vanquished their fathers thirty years before about the smell. That was two years after her father's death and a short time after her sweetheart – the one we believed would marry her – had deserted her. After her father's death she went out very little; after her sweetheart went away, people hardly saw her at all. A few of the ladies had the temerity to call, but were not received, and the only sign of life about the place was the Negro man – a young man then – going in and out with a market basket.

"Just as if a man – any man – could keep a kitchen properly," the ladies said; so they were not surprised when the smell developed. It was another link between the gross, teeming world and the high and mighty Griersons.

A neighbor, a woman, complained to the mayor, Judge Stevens, eighty years old.

"But what will you have me do about it, madam?" he said.

"Why, send her word to stop it," the woman said. "Isn't there a law?"

"I'm sure that won't be necessary," Judge Stevens said. "It's probably just a snake or a rat that nigger of hers killed in the yard. I'll speak to him about it."

The next day he received two more complaints, one from a man who came in diffident deprecation. "We really must do something about it, Judge. I'd be the last one in the world to bother Miss Emily, but we've got to do something." That night the Board of Aldermen met – three graybeards and one younger man, a member of the rising generation.

"It's simple enough," he said. "Send her word to have her place cleaned up. Give her a certain time to do it in, and if she don't ..."

"Dammit, sir," Judge Stevens said, "will you accuse a lady to her face of smelling bad?"

So the next night, after midnight, four men crossed Miss Emily's lawn and slunk about the house like burglars, sniffing along the base of the brick-work and at the cellar openings while one of them performed a regular sowing motion with his hand out of a sack slung from his shoulder. They broke open the cellar door and sprinkled lime there, and in all the outbuild-ings. As they recrossed the lawn, a window that had been dark was lighted and Miss Emily sat in it, the light behind her, and her upright torso motion-less as that of an idol. They crept quietly across the lawn and into the shadow of the locusts that lined the street. After a week or two the smell went away.

That was when people had begun to feel really sorry for her. People in our town, remembering how old lady Wyatt, her great-aunt, had gone completely crazy at last, believed that the Griersons held themselves a little too high for what they really were. None of the young men were quite good enough for Miss Emily and such. We had long thought of them as a tableau, Miss Emily a slender figure in white in the background, her father a spraddled silhouette in the foreground, his back to her and clutching a horsewhip, the two of them framed by the back-flung front door. So when she got to be thirty and was still single, we were not please exactly, but vindicated; even with insanity in the family she wouldn't have turned down all of her chances if they had really materialized.

When her father died, it got about that the house was all that was left to her; and in a way, people were glad. At last they could pity Miss Emily. Being left alone, and a pauper, she had become humanized. Now she too would know the old thrill and the old despair of a penny more or less.

The day after his death all the ladies prepared to call at the house and offer condolence and aid, as is our custom. Miss Emily met them at the door, dressed as usual and with no trace of grief on her face. She told them that her father was not dead. She did that for three days, with the ministers calling on her, and the doctors, trying to persuade her to let them dispose of the body. Just as they were about to resort to law and force, she broke down, and they buried her father quickly.

We did not say she was crazy then. We believed she had to do that. We remembered all the young men her father had driven away, and we knew that with nothing left, she would have to cling to that which had robbed her, as people will.

III

She was sick for a long time. When we saw her again, her hair was cut short, making her look like a girl, with a vague resemblance to those angels in colored church windows – sort of tragic and serene.

The town had just let the contracts for paving the sidewalks, and in the summer after her father's death they began the work. The construction company came with niggers and mules and machinery, and a foreman named Homer Barron, a Yankee – a big, dark, ready man, with a big voice and eyes lighter than his face. The little boys would follow in groups to hear him cuss the niggers, and the niggers singing in time to the rise and fall of picks. Pretty soon he knew everybody in town. Whenever you heard a lot of laughing anywhere about the square, Homer Barron would be in the center of the group. Presently we began to see him and Miss Emily on Sunday afternoons driving in the yellow-wheeled buggy and the matched team of bays from the livery stable.

At first we were glad that Miss Emily would have an interest, because the ladies all said, "Of course a Grierson would not think seriously of a Northerner, a day laborer." But there were still others, older people, who said that even grief could not cause a real lady to forget *noblesse oblige* – without calling it *noblesse oblige*. They just said, "Poor Emily. Her kinsfolk should come to her." She had some kin in Alabama; but years ago her father had fallen out with them over the estate of old lady Wyatt, the crazy woman, and there was no communication between the two families. They had not even been represented at the funeral.

And as soon as the old people said, "Poor Emily," the whispering began. "Do you suppose it's really so?" they said to one another. "Of course it is. What else could ..." This behind their hands; rustling of craned silk and satin behind jalousies closed upon the sun of Sunday afternoon as the thin, swift clop-clop-clop of the matched team passed: "Poor Emily."

She carried her head high enough – even when we believed that she was fallen. It was as if she demanded more than ever the recognition of her dignity as the last Grierson; as if it had wanted that touch of earthiness to reaffirm her imperviousness. Like when she bought the rat poison, the arsenic. That was over a year after they had begun to say "Poor Emily," and while the two female cousins were visiting her.

"I want some poison," she said to the druggist. She was over thirty then, still a slight woman, though thinner than usual, with cold, haughty black eyes in a face the flesh of which was strained across the temples and about the eye-sockets as you imagine a lighthouse-keeper's face ought to look. "I want some poison," she said.

"Yes, Miss Emily. What kind? For rats and such? I'd recom –"

"I want the best you have. I don't care what kind."

The druggist named several. "They'll kill anything up to an elephant. But what you want is –"

"Arsenic," Miss Emily said. "Is that a good one?"

"Is ... arsenic? Yes, ma'am. But what you want –"

"I want arsenic."

The druggist looked down at her. She looked back at him, erect, her face like a strained flag. "Why, of course," the druggist said. "If that's what you want. But the law requires you to tell what you are going to use it for."

Miss Emily just stared at him, her head tilted back in order to look him eye for eye, until he looked away and went and got the arsenic and wrapped it up. The Negro delivery boy brought her the package; the druggist didn't come back. When she opened the package at home there was written on the box, under the skull and bones: "For rats."

IV

So the next day we all said, "She will kill herself"; and we said it would be the best thing. When she had first begun to be seen with Homer Barron, we had said, "She will marry him." Then we said, "She will persuade him yet," because Homer himself had remarked – he liked men, and it was known that he drank with the younger men in the Elk's Club – that he was not a marrying man. Later we said, "Poor Emily" behind the jalousies as they passed on Sunday afternoon in the glittering buggy, Miss Emily with her head high and Homer Barron with his hat cocked and a cigar in his teeth, reins and whip in a yellow glove.

Then some of the ladies began to say that it was a disgrace to the town, and a bad example to the young people. The men did not want to interfere, but at last the ladies forced the Baptist minister – Miss Emily's people were Episcopal – to call upon her. He would never divulge what happened during that interview, but he refused to go back again. The next Sunday they again drove about the streets, and the following day the minister's wife wrote to Miss Emily's relations in Alabama.

So she had blood-kin under her roof again and we sat back to watch developments. At first nothing happened. Then we were sure they were to be married. We learned that Miss Emily had been to the jeweler's and or-dered a man's toilet set in silver, with the letters H.B. on each piece. Two days later we learned that she had bought a complete outfit of men's clothing, including a nightshirt, and we said, "They are married." We were really glad. We were glad because the two female cousins were even more Grierson than Miss Emily had ever been.

So we were not surprised when Homer Barron – the streets had been finished some time since – was gone. We were a little disappointed that there was not a public blowing-off, but we believed that he had gone on to prepare for Miss Emily's coming, or to give her a chance to get rid of the cousins. (By that time it was a cabal, and we were all Miss Emily's allies to help circumvent the cousins.) Sure enough, after another week they de-parted. And, as we had expected all along, within three days Homer Barron was back in town. A neighbor saw the Negro man admit him at the kitchen door at dusk one evening.

And that was the last we saw of Homer Barron. And of Miss Emily for some time. The Negro man went in and out with the market basket, but the front door remained closed. Now and then we would see her at a window for a moment, as the men did that night when they sprinkled the lime, but for almost six months she did not appear on the streets. Then we knew that this was to be expected too; as if that quality of her father which had thwarted her woman's life so many times had been too virulent and too furious to die.

When we next saw Miss Emily, she had grown fat and her hair was turning gray. During the next few years it grew grayer and grayer until it attained an even pepper-and-salt iron-gray, when it ceased turning. Up to the day of her death at seventy-four it was still that vigorous iron-gray, like the hair of an active man.

From that time on her front door remained closed, save for a period of six or seven years, when she was about forty, during which she gave lessons in china-painting. She fitted up a studio in one of the downstairs rooms, where the daughters and grand-daughters of Colonel Sartoris' contemporaries were sent to her with the same regularity and in the same spirit that they were sent to church on Sundays, with a twenty-five cent piece for the collection plate. Meanwhile her taxes had been remitted.

The newer generation became the backbone and the spirit of the town, and the painting pupils grew up and fell away and did not send their children to her with boxes of color and tedious brushes and pictures cut from the ladies' magazines. The front door closed upon the last one and remained closed for good. When the town got free postal delivery, Miss Emily alone refused to let them fasten the metal numbers above her door and attach a mailbox to it. She would not listen to them.

Daily, monthly, yearly we watched the Negro grow grayer and more stooped, going in and out with the market basket. Each December we sent her a tax notice, which would be returned by the post office a week later, unclaimed. Now and then we would see her in one of the downstairs windows – she had evidently shut up the top floor of the house – like the carven torso of an idol in a niche, looking or not looking at us, we could never tell which. Thus she passed from generation to generation – dear, inescapable, impervious, tranquil, and perverse.

And so she died. Fell ill in the house filled with dust and shadows, with only a doddering Negro man to wait on her. We did not even know she was sick; we had long since given up trying to get any information from the Negro. He talked to no one, probably not even to her, for his voice had grown harsh and rusty, as if from disuse.

She died in one of the downstairs rooms, in a heavy walnut bed with a curtain, her gray head propped on a pillow yellow and moldy with age and lack of sunlight.

V

The Negro met the first of the ladies at the front door and let them in, with their hushed, sibilant voices and their quick, curious glances, and then he disappeared. He walked right through the house and out the back and was not seen again.

The two female cousins came at once. They held the funeral on the second day, with the town coming to look at Miss Emily beneath a mass of bought flowers, with the crayon face of her father musing profoundly above the bier and the ladies sibilant and macabre; and the very old men – some in their brushed Confederate uniforms – on the porch and the lawn, talking of Miss Emily as if she had been a contemporary of theirs, believing that they had danced with her and courted her perhaps, confusing time with the mathematical progression, as the old do, to whom all the past is not a di-minishing road but, instead, a huge meadow which no winter ever quite touches, divided from them now by the narrow bottleneck of the most recent decade of years.

Already we knew that there was one room in that region above stairs which no one had seen in forty years, and which would have to be forced. They waited until Miss Emily was decently in the ground before they opened it.

The violence of breaking down the door seemed to fill this room with pervading dust. A thin, acrid pall as of the tomb seemed to lie everywhere upon this room decked and furnished as for a bridal: upon the valance cur-tains of faded rose color, upon the rose-shaded lights, upon the dressing table, upon the delicate array of crystal and the man's toilet things backed with tarnished silver, silver so tarnished that the monogram was obscured. Among them lay a collar and tie, as if they had just been removed, which, lifted, left upon the surface a pale crescent in the dust. Upon a chair hung the suit, carefully folded; beneath it the two mute shoes and the discarded socks.

The man himself lay in the bed.

For a long while we just stood there, looking down at the profound and fleshless grin. The body had apparently once lain in the attitude of an embrace, but now the long sleep that outlasts love, that conquers even the grimace of love, had cuckolded him. What was left of him, rotted beneath what was left of the nightshirt, had become inextricable from the bed in which he lay; and upon him and upon the pillow beside him lay that even coating of the patient and biding dust.

Then we noticed that in the second pillow was the indentation of a head. One of us lifted something from it, and leaning forward, that faint and invisible dust dry and acrid in the nostrils, we saw a long strand of iron-gray hair.

EXERCISE 1

Discuss the following questions:

1. How powerful is Miss Emily? Insofar as she has power/authority, what does it consist of?
2. How would you characterize the narrator? What is his attitude toward Miss Emily? Do you share it?
3. Some readers find Miss Emily monstrous and are appalled by her; others see her as a victim and pity her. What is your perception of Miss Emily and how do you feel about her?
4. Why is Miss Emily referred to as "Miss"? On the whole, titles are a mark of status (e.g. Dr., Lady, Judge). How does Miss Emily's title function in the story?
5. Why do you think Faulkner entitled his story "A Rose for Emily"? In what ways might the title affect the way we read the text?
6. Some critics view Miss Emily as a protagonist whose sex is of secondary importance; others emphasize the fact that she is a woman. Which view do you find more helpful in constructing your interpretation of the story?

EXERCISE 2

1. After you have discussed the story in terms of the above questions, read the following critical statements about Faulkner's story. Note your agreements and disagreements with the points made.

Cleanth Brooks and Robert Penn Warren:
Understanding Fiction (excerpt)

This is a story of horror. We have a decaying mansion in which the protagonist, shut away from the world, grows into something monstrous, and becomes as divorced from the human as some fungus growing in the dark on a damp wall. Miss Emily Grierson remains in voluntary isolation (or perhaps fettered by some inner compulsion) away from the bustle and dust and sunshine of the human world of normal affairs, and what in the end is found in the upstairs room gives perhaps a sense of penetrating and gruesome horror.

Has this sense of horror been conjured up for its own sake? It not, then why has the author contrive to insert so much of the monstrous into the story? In other words, does the horror contribute to the theme of Faulkner's story? Is the horror meaningful?

In order to answer this question, we shall have to examine rather carefully some of the items earlier in the story. In the first place, why does Miss Emily commit her monstrous act? Is she supplied with a proper motivation? Faulkner has, we can see, been rather careful to prepare for his dénouement. Miss Emily, it becomes obvious fairly early in the story, is one of those persons for whom the distinction between reality and illusion has blurred out. For example, she refuses to admit that she owes any taxes. When the mayor protests, she does not recognize him as mayor. Instead, she refers the committee to Colonel Sartoris, who, as the reader is told, has been dead for nearly ten years. For Miss Emily, apparently, Colonel Sartoris is still alive. Most specific preparation of all, when her father dies, she denies to the townspeople for three days that he is dead: "Just as they were about to resort to law and force, she broke down, and they buried her father quickly."

Miss Emily is obviously a pathological case. The narrator indicates plainly enough that people felt that she was crazy. All of this explanation prepares us for what Miss Emily does in order to hold her lover – the dead lover is in one sense still alive for her – the realms of reality and appearance merge. But having said this, we have got no nearer to justifying the story; for, if Faulkner is merely interested in relating a case history of abnormal psychology, the story lacks meaning and justification as a story and we are back to fiction as "clinical report"... If the story is to be justified, there must be what may be called a moral significance, a meaning in moral terms – not merely psychological terms.

Incidentally, it is very easy to misread the story as merely a horrible case history, presented in order to titillate the reader. Faulkner has been frequently judged to be doing nothing more than this in his work.

The lapse of the distinction between illusion and reality, between life and death, is important, therefore, in helping to account for Miss Emily's motivation, but merely to note this lapse is not fully to account for the theme of the story.

Suppose we approach the motivation again in these terms: what is Miss Emily like? What are the mainsprings of her character? What causes the distinction between illusion and reality to blur out for her? She is obviously a woman of tremendous firmness of will. In the matter of the taxes, crazed though she is, she is never at a loss. She is utterly composed. She dominates the rather frightened committee of officers who see her. In the matter of her purchase of the poison, she completely overawes the clerk. She makes no pretense. She refuses to tell him what she wants the poison for. And yet this firmness of will and this iron pride have not kept her from being thwarted and hurt. Her father has run off the young men who came to call upon her, and for the man who tells the story, Miss Emily and her father form a tableau: "Miss Emily a slender figure in white in the background, her father a spraddled silhouette in the foreground, his back to her and clutching a horsewhip, the two of them framed by the back-flung front door." Whether the picture is a remembered scene, or merely a symbolical construct, this is the picture which remains in the storyteller's mind.

We have indicated that her pride is connected with her contempt for public opinion. This comes to the fore, of course, when she rides around about the town with the foreman whom everybody believes is beneath her. And it is her proud refusal to admit an external set of codes, or conventions, or other wills which contradict her own will, which makes her capable at the end of keeping her lover from going away. Confronted with his jilting her, she tries to override not only his will and the opinion of other people, but the laws of death and decay themselves.

But this, still, hardly gives the meaning of the story. For in all that has been said thus far, we are still merely accounting for a psychological aberration – we are still merely dealing with a case history in abnormal psychology. In order to make a case for the story as "meaningful," we shall have to tie Miss Emily's thoughts and actions back into the normal life of the community, and establish some sort of relationship between them. And just here one pervasive element in the narration suggests a clue. The story is told by one of the townspeople. And in it, as a constant factor, is the reference to what the community thought of Miss Emily. Continually through the story is it what "we" said, and then what "we" did, and what seemed true to "us," and so on. The narrator puts the matter even more sharply still. He says, in the course of the story, that to the community Miss Emily seemed "dear, inescapable, impervious, tranquil, and perverse." Each of the adjectives is important and meaningful. In a sense, Miss Emily because of her very fact of isolation and perversity belongs to the whole community. She is even something treasured by it. Ironically, because of Emily's perversion of an aristocratic independence of mores and because of her contempt for "what people say," her life is public, even communal. And various phrases used by the narrator underline this view of her position. For example, her face looks "as you imagine a lighthouse-keeper's face ought to look," like the face of a person who lives in the kind of isolation imposed on a lighthouse-keeper, who looks out into the blackness and whose light serves a public function. Or, again, after her father's death, she becomes very ill, and when she appears after the illness, she has "a vague resemblance to those angels in colored church windows – sort of tragic and serene." Whatever we make of these descriptions, certainly the author is trying to suggest a kind of calm and dignity which is super-mundane, unearthly, or "over-earthly," such as an angel might possess.

Miss Emily, then, is a combination of idol and scapegoat for the community. On the one hand, the community feels admiration for Miss Emily – she represents something in the past of the community which the community is proud of. They feel a sort of awe of her, as is illustrated by the behavior of the mayor and the committee in her presence. On the other hand, her queerness, the fact that she cannot compete with them in their ordinary life, the fact that she is hopelessly out of touch with the modern world – all of these things make them feel superior to her, and also to that past which she represents. It is, then, Miss Emily's complete detachment which gives her actions their special meaning for the community.

Miss Emily, since she is the conscious aristocrat, since she is consciously "better" than other people, since she is above and outside their canons of behavior, can, at the same time, be worse than other people; and she *is* worse, horribly so. She is worse than other people, but at the same time, as the narrator implies, she remains somehow admirable. This raises a fundamental question: why is this true?

Perhaps the horrible and the admirable aspects of Miss Emily's final deed arise from the same basic fact of her character: she insists on meeting the world on her own terms. She never cringes, she never begs for sympathy, she refuses to shrink into an amiable old maid, she never accepts the community's ordinary judgments or values. This independence of spirit and pride can, and does in her case, twist the individual into a sort of monster, but, at the same time, this refusal to accept the herd values carries with it a dignity and courage. The community senses this, as we gather from the fact that the community carries out the decencies of the funeral before breaking in the door of the upper room. There is, as it were, a kind of secret understanding that she has won her right of privacy, until she herself has entered history. Furthermore, despite the fact that, as the narrator says, "already we knew that there was one room in that region above stairs which no one had seen in forty years, and which would have to be forced," her funeral is something of a state occasion, with "the very old men – some in their brushed Confederate uniforms – on the porch and the lawn, talking of Miss Emily as if she had been a contemporary of theirs, believing that they had danced with her and courted her perhaps ..." In other words, the community accepts her into its honored history. All of this works as a kind of tacit recognition of Miss Emily's triumph of will. The community, we are told earlier, had wanted to pity Miss Emily when she had lost her money, just as they had wanted to commiserate over her when they believed that she had actually become a fallen woman, but she had triumphed over their pity and commiseration and condemnation, just as she had triumphed over all their other attitudes.

But, as we have indicated earlier, it may be said that Miss Emily is mad. This may be true, but there are two things to consider in this connection. First, one must consider the special terms which her "madness" takes. Her madness is simply a development of her pride and her refusal so submit to ordinary standards of behavior. So, because of this fact, her "madness" is meaningful after all. It involves issues which in themselves are really important and have to do with the world of conscious moral choice. Second, the community interprets her "madness" as meaningful. They admire her, even if they are disappointed by her refusals to let herself be pitied, and the narrator, who is a spokesman for the community, recognizes the last grim revelation as an instance of her having carried her own values to their ultimate conclusion. She would marry the common laborer, Homer Barron, let the community think what it would. She would not be jilted. And she would hold him as a lover. But it would all be on her own terms. She remains completely dominant, and contemptuous of the day-to-day world.

It has been suggested by many critics that tragedy implies a hero who is completely himself, who insists on meeting the world on his own terms, who wants something so intensely, or lives so intensely, that he cannot accept any compromise. It cannot be maintained that this story is comparable to any of the great tragedies, such as *Hamlet* or *King Lear,* but it can be pointed out that this story, in its own way, involves some of the same basic elements. Certainly, Miss Emily's pride, isolation, and independence remind one of factors in the character of the typical tragic hero. And it can be pointed out that, just as the horror of her deed lies outside the ordinary life of the community, so the magnificence of her independence lies outside its ordinary virtues.

From Cleanth Brooks and Robert Penn Warren, *Understanding Fiction,* © 1979, pp. 227–31. Reprinted by permission of Prentice Hall, Upper Saddle River, NJ.

Robert Crosman: "How Readers Make Meaning"

For a number of years now I have been arguing that readers make the meanings of literary texts, and that accordingly there is no such thing as "right reading." Such a conclusion troubles most students of literature, and raises a host of questions, some of which – like "By what authority can I tell a student his interpretation is wrong?" or "How then can English be called a discipline?" – are questions of campus politics that are, theoretically at least, very easily answered. The problem for us is to answer the much more complex question of *how* readers make meaning: under what impulses or constraints, following what conventions or strategies? Beyond this lies a second thorny question: are different readers' results all equally valid?

I want to try answering these general questions by looking at a specific text – William Faulkner's short story "A Rose for Emily" – and two antithetical interpretations of it. My contention is that although these interpretations contradict each other, both are valid. How this can be, it will be my task to explain. The two readers are myself and one of the students in a course called "Response to Literature" that I taught at Trinity College in 1976. Our procedure was to read a text, and then immediately to write in our journals about our thoughts, feelings, and fantasies during and after reading. Here first is my journal entry, warts and all, exactly as I wrote it:

This is a story I had never actually read, though I had heard of it, read something about it, and in particular knew its ending, which kept me from feeling the pure shock that the reader must feel who knows nothing of what is coming. Even so I felt a shock, and reacted with an audible cry of mingled loathing and pleasure at the final and most shocking discovery: that Emily has slept with this cadaver for forty years. The loathing is easy enough to explain; the problem is to explain the pleasure. But before trying, let me record other parts of my "response."

I found my mind wandering as I read this story; there were paragraphs I had to reread several times. For one reason or another I was "uninvolved" with the story, perhaps a product of the circumstances under which I read it, but possibly also a response to the story itself. There are various reasons why I might tonight shun wrestling with a "serious" story, but perhaps I also shrank from the "horror" I knew was coming. Perhaps the story of a woman killing her faithless lover is not one I particularly want to hear. I've known about this story for years, yet had no urge to read it, perhaps because I knew what it contained.

She kills him. What do I care about him? – he's hardly in the story at all. But I noticed the repeated differentiation at the story's beginning between men and women, and the put-downs of women. The story seemed to be setting me up for some attitude toward women, and even though I noticed this, I did take the attitude: women are mean, ill-willed, and therefore (though not men's equals) menacing. Miss Emily is menacing. But at first she seems grotesque and stupid: her house smells bad; she's fat, with a dead look; she faces down the fathers [i.e. the aldermen] by (apparently) missing their point. Only gradually do I see the force of her will, that just because she doesn't go out or *do* anything doesn't mean that she isn't in control.

The scene with the rat-poison is crucial here: Miss Emily got her way, and the fact that her way is inscrutable, though surely menacing (arsenic), only makes it worse. The whole feeling of the story is of a mystery, something to do with male-female relationships, as well as time, perhaps, but a mystery one doesn't entirely want solved. Perhaps because I knew what was coming my mind wandered, putting even further distance between myself and the disgusting (but fascinating) revelation of the "bedroom" scene at the end. But the distancing is there in the story itself. The time-lags, the mysteriousness, the indirection, all put barriers between you and the story's subject.

So this is what I'd say at first reading, anyway. As far as response goes, mine is a considerable *fear* of the discovery I know is waiting, the sex-and-death thing, though there is a *fascination*, too. As far as the story's technique goes, I think it sets up shields of various sorts, that hide the ultimate truth, yet that have chinks that give us inklings, and the effect of secrets-not-entirely-hidden, or horrible-premonitions-defended-against, is what I'd guess is the technique that seems to arouse my feelings.

Now let me admit, right off, that this isn't an "unmediated" response to Faulkner's story. It was written not during but immediately after reading the story, by a relatively sophisticated, self-conscious reader, who also had some foreknowledge of the story's shocking climax. Most of all, it is a *written account* of a response, and so subject to all kinds of misrepresentation on my part *as I wrote it*. Also it was written by someone who has had considerable exposure to psychotherapy, and who therefore is somewhat at ease when expressing a taboo pleasure of contemplating necrophilia, an activity that is widely considered (and no doubt really is) loathsome to engage in.

Nonetheless, all this said, my response should give comfort to literary Freudians. For what I saw in "A Rose for Emily" was pretty certainly a "primal scene." Both my fear and my interest, my loathing and pleasure, derived, at least in part, from remembered childish speculation as to what went on in the parental bedroom. The structure of the story's plot is to set up a dark and impenetrable mystery – what is troubling Emily? – and to penetrate deeper and deeper into her past in hopes of getting an answer. Formally the pleasure is derived from solving the mystery, but the solution is a shocking one. My unconscious *knew* all along that nothing good went on behind a locked bedroom door, but now it has proof, and has won a victory over my conscious mind, which assured me it was none of my business. My conscious mind, meanwhile, has to content itself with solving a puzzle, with the self-evident reflection that after all Emily and Homer aren't Mom and Dad, and that, anyway, "it's only a story."

Beyond the illicit pleasure of letting a taboo thought become momentarily conscious, there was more bad news for my conscious mind in my response to "A Rose for Emily," for it turns out that my unconscious is a nasty little sexist, as I dutifully though rather reluctantly reported in my journal: "women are mean, ill-willed, men's inferiors, and menacing." I don't approve of such feelings, or consciously agree with them – some of my best friends are women – but they are *there* lying in wait for me when I read Faulkner. My shocked response to the imagined scene of Emily bedding down with Homer Barron's decomposing body, and my related interest at male/female antagonism and conflict in the story are only the beginnings of an interpretation, of course, but any class I would teach, or essay I would write on the story would feature such interests prominently.

In sharp contrast to my response was that of my student, Stacy. Since her notebook remained in her possession, I will summarize from memory her entry on "A Rose for Emily." Surprisingly, Stacy did not mention the terrible denouement of the story – the discovery of Homer Barron's remains in Emily's bed. On questioning, she said that Emily's poisoning of Homer remained shadowy and hypothetical in her mind, and she had completely missed the implication of the strand of Emily's hair found on the pillow next to the corpse. Instead, Stacy had written a rather poetic reverie about her *grandmother,* of whom she was strongly reminded by Emily. The grandmother lived, Stacy wrote, shut away in a house full of relics and mementos of the past. Events of long ago, and people long dead, were more real to her than the world of the present, but Stacy found very positive things in her grandmother, and (by implication) in Emily as well: endurance, faith, love. She even identified the frail, pretty woman with Faulkner's picture of Emily when young: "a slender figure in white."

The contrast between our two reactions to the story was striking, and cause for discussion in class. In a more conventional course, I might have been tearing my hair over a student who so "missed the point" of the story as to ignore in her interpretation the terrifying climax of Emily's story, and who did not even notice the grizzly implications of that strand of iron-grey hair on the pillow beside Homer Barron. But what I found myself doing, instead, was to go back over the story and see how much of its meaning *I* had missed, how much there was in Faulkner's picture of Emily that *was* attractive, noble, tragic. Deprived of all normal suitors by a domineering father, she had clung to that father, even in death; deprived of her father, she had found a suitor outside the limits of respectability for a woman of her class and background; threatened with his loss as well she found a way to keep him, and then she remained true to him all the days of her life. Certainly it is hard entirely to like a Juliet who poisons her Romeo, yet remember that this is an extraordinarily evasive, indirect story, in which the reader can easily overlook unwanted implications. No poisoning actually occurs in its pages; the deed is left for the reader to infer. Stacy found it easy to ignore, and when confronted with it, accepted it as a qualification, but not a refutation of her admiration for Emily: just as I was able to modify my interpretation of the story without giving up my spontaneous horror, so Stacy could acknowledge the horror, without surrendering her view of Emily as embodying positive values.

From *College Literature* 9 (1982), pp. 207–15. Reprinted by permission of *College Literature*.

Judith Fetterley: *The Resisting Reader. A Feminist Approach to American Fiction* (excerpts)

[from Introduction]
Though the grotesque may serve Faulkner as a disguise in the same way that the ideal serves Hawthorne, "A Rose for Emily" goes farther than "The Birthmark" in making the power of men over women an overt subject. Emily's life is shaped by her father's absolute control over her; her murder of Homer Barron is *re*action, not action. Though Emily exercises the power the myths of sexism make available to her, that power is minimal; her retaliation is no alternative to the patriarchy which oppresses her. Yet Faulkner, like Anderson and Hawthorne, ultimately protects himself and short-circuits the implications of his analysis, not simply through the use of the grotesque, which makes Emily eccentric rather than central, but also through his choice of her victim. In having Emily murder Homer Barron, a northern day-laborer, rather than Judge Stevens, the southern patriarch, Faulkner indicates how far he is willing to go in imagining even the minimal reversal of power involved in retaliation. The elimination of Homer Barron is no

real threat to the system Judge Stevens represents. Indeed, a few day-labor-
ers may have to be sacrificed here and there to keep that system going....

A Rose for "A Rose for Emily"

[from Chapter 1]

In "A Rose for Emily" the grotesque reality implicit in Aylmer's idealiza-
tion of Georgiana becomes explicit. Justifying Faulkner's use of the grotesque has been a major concern of critics who have written on the story. If,
however, one approaches "A Rose for Emily" from a feminist perspective,
one notices that the grotesque aspects of the story are a result of its violation of the expectations generated by the conventions of sexual politics.
The ending shocks us not simply by its hint of necrophilia; more shocking
is the fact that it is a woman who provides the hint. It is one thing for Poe to
spend his nights in the tomb of Annabel Lee and another thing for Miss
Emily Grierson to deposit a strand of iron-gray hair on the pillow beside the
rotted corpse of Homer Barron. Further, we do not expect to discover that a
woman has murdered a man. The conventions of sexual politics have famil-
iarized us with the image of Georgiana nobly accepting death at her husband's hand. To reverse this "natural" pattern inevitably produces the grotesque.

Faulkner, however, is not interested in invoking the kind of grotesque
which is the consequence of reversing the clichés of sexism for the sake of
a cheap thrill; that is left to writers like Mickey Spillane. (Indeed, Spillane's
ready willingness to capitalize on the shock value provided by the image of
woman as killer in *I, the Jury* suggests, by contrast, how little such a sexist
gambit is Faulkner's intent.) Rather, Faulkner invokes the grotesque in
order to illuminate and define the true nature of the conventions on which it
depends. "A Rose for Emily" is a story not of a conflict between the South
and the North or between the old order and the new; it is a story of the patriarchy North and South, new and old, and of the sexual conflict within it. As
Faulkner himself has implied,[1] it is a story of a woman victimized and
betrayed by the system of sexual politics, who nevertheless has discovered,
within the structures that victimize her, sources of power for herself. If
"The Birthmark" is the story of how to murder your wife and get away with
it, "A Rose for Emily" is the story of how to murder your gentleman caller
and get away with it. Faulkner's story is an analysis of how men's attitudes
toward women turn back upon themselves; it is a demonstration of the the-
sis that it is impossible to oppress without in turn being oppressed, it is
impossible to kill without creating the conditions for your own murder. "A

Rose for Emily" is the story of a *lady* and of her revenge for that grotesque identity.

"When Miss Emily Grierson died, our whole town went to her funeral." The public and communal nature of Emily's funeral, a festival that brings the town together, clarifying its social relationships and revitalizing its sense of the past, indicates her central role in Jefferson. Alive, Emily is town property and the subject of shared speculation; dead, she is town history and the subject of legend. It is her value as a symbol, however obscure and however ambivalent, of something that is of central significance to the identity of Jefferson and to the meaning of its history that compels the narrator to assume a communal voice to tell her story. For Emily, like Georgiana, is a man-made object, a cultural artifact, and what she is reflects and defines the culture that has produced her.

The history the narrator relates to us reveals Jefferson's continuous emotional involvement with Emily. Indeed, though she shuts herself up in a house which she rarely leaves and which no one enters, her furious isolation is in direct proportion to the town's obsession with her. Like Georgiana, she is the object of incessant attention; her every act is immediately consumed by the town for gossip and seized on to justify their interference in her affairs. Her private life becomes a public document that the town folk feel free to interpret at will, and they are alternately curious, jealous, spiteful, pitying, partisan, proud, disapproving, admiring, and vindicated. Her funeral is not simply a communal ceremony; it is also the climax of their invasion of her private life and the logical extension of their voyeuristic attitude toward her. Despite the narrator's demurral, getting inside Emily's house is the all-consuming desire of the town's population, both male and female; while the men may wait a little longer, their motive is still prurient curiosity: "Already we knew that there was one room in that region above stairs which no one had seen in forty years, and which would have to be forced. They waited until Miss Emily was decently in the ground before they opened it."

In a context in which the overtones of violation and invasion are so palpable, the word "decently" has that ironic ring which gives the game away. When the men finally do break down the door, they find that Emily has satisfied their prurience with a vengeance and in doing so has created for them a mirror image of themselves. The true nature of Emily's relation to Jefferson is contained in the analogies between what those who break open that room see in it and what has brought them there to see it. The perverse, violent, and grotesque aspects of the sight of Homer Barron's rotted corpse in a room decked out for a bridal and now faded and covered in dust reflects back to them the perverseness of their own prurient interest in Emily, the

violence implicit in their continued invasions of her life, and the grotesqueness of the symbolic artifact they have made of her – their monument, their
idol, their lady. Thus, the figure that Jefferson places at the center of its
legendary history does indeed contain the clue to the meaning of that history – a history which began long before Emily's funeral and long before
Homer Barron's disappearance or appearance and long before Colonel
Sartoris' fathering of edicts and remittances. It is recorded in that emblem
which lies at the heart of the town's memory and at the heart of patriarchal
culture: "We had long thought of them as a tableau, Miss Emily a slender
figure in white in the background, her father a spraddled silhouette in the
foreground, his back to her and clutching a horsewhip, the two of them
framed by the back-flung front door."

The importance of Emily's father in shaping the quality of her life is
insistent throughout the story. Even in her death the force of his presence is
felt; above her dead body sits "the crayon face of her father musing profoundly," symbolic of the degree to which he has dominated and shadowed
her life, "as if that quality of her father which had thwarted her woman's
life so many times had been too virulent and too furious to die." The violence of this consuming relationship is made explicit in the imagery of the
tableau. Although the violence is apparently directed outward – the up-
raised horsewhip against the would-be suitor – the real object of it is the
woman-daughter, forced into the background and dominated by the phallic
figure of the spraddled father whose back is turned on her and who prevents
her from getting out at the same time that he prevents them from getting in.
Like Georgiana's spatial confinement in "The Birthmark," Emily's is a
metaphor for her psychic confinement: her identity is determined by the
constructs of her father's mind, and she can no more escape from his creation of her as "a slender figure in white" than she can escape his house.

What is true for Emily in relation to her father is equally true for her in
relation to Jefferson: her status as a lady is a cage from which she cannot
escape. To them she is always *Miss* Emily; she is never referred to and
never thought of as otherwise. In omitting her title from his, Faulkner
emphasizes the point that the real violence done to Emily is in making her a
"Miss"; the omission is one of his roses for her. Because she is *Miss* Emily
Grierson, Emily's father dresses her in white, places her in the background,
and drives away her suitors. Because she is Miss Emily Grierson, the town
invests her with that communal significance which makes her the object of
their obsession and the subject of their incessant scrutiny. And because she
is a lady, the town is able to impose a particular code of behavior on her
("But there were still others, older people, who said that even grief could

not cause a real lady to forget *noblesse oblige*") and to see in her failure to live up to that code an excuse for interfering in her life. As a lady, Emily is venerated, but veneration results in the more telling emotions of envy and spite: "It was another link between the gross, teeming world and the high and mighty Griersons"; "People ... believed that the Griersons held themselves a little too high for what they really were." The violence implicit in the desire to see the monument fall and reveal itself for clay suggests the violence inherent in the original impulse to venerate.

The violence behind veneration is emphasized through another telling emblem in the story. Emily's position as an hereditary obligation upon the town dates from "that day in 1894 when Colonel Sartoris, the mayor – he who fathered the edict that no Negro woman should appear on the streets without an apron on – remitted her taxes, the dispensation dating from the death of her father on into perpetuity." The conjunction of these two actions in the same syntactic unit is crucial, for it insists on their essential similarity. It indicates that the impulse to exempt is analogous to the desire to restrict, and that what appears to be a kindness or an act of veneration is in fact an insult. Sartoris' remission of Emily's taxes is a public declaration of the fact that a lady is not considered to be, and hence not allowed or enabled to be, economically independent (consider, in this connection, Emily's lessons in china painting; they are a latter-day version of Sartoris' "charity" and a brilliant image of Emily's economic uselessness). His act is a public statement of the fact that a lady, if she is to survive, must have either husband or father, and that, because Emily has neither, the town must assume responsibility for her. The remission of taxes that defines Emily's status dates from the death of her father, and she is handed over from one patron to the next, the town instead of husband taking on the role of father. Indeed, the use of the word "fathered" in describing Sartoris' behavior as mayor underlines the fact that his chivalric attitude toward Emily is simply a subtler and more dishonest version of her father's horsewhip.

The narrator is the last of the patriarchs who take upon themselves the burden of defining Emily's life, and his violence toward her is the most subtle of all. His tone of incantatory reminiscence and nostalgic veneration seems free of the taint of horsewhip and edict. Yet a thoroughgoing contempt for the "ladies" who spy and pry and gossip out of their petty jealousy and curiosity is one of the clearest strands in the narrator's consciousness. Emily is exempted from the general indictment because she is a *real* lady – that is, eccentric, slightly crazy, obsolete, a "stubborn and coquettish decay," absurd but indulged; "dear, inescapable, impervious, tranquil, and perverse"; indeed, anything and everything but human.

Not only does "A Rose for Emily" expose the violence done to a woman by making her a lady; it also explores the particular form of power the victim gains from this position and can use on those who enact this violence. "A Rose for Emily" is concerned with the consequences of violence for both the violated and the violators. One of the most striking aspects of the story is the disparity between Miss Emily Grierson and the Emily to whom Faulkner gives his rose in ironic imitation of the chivalric behavior the story exposes. The form of Faulkner's title establishes a camaraderie between author and protagonist and signals that a distinction must be made between the story Faulkner is telling and the story the narrator is telling. This distinction is of major importance because it suggests, of course, that the narrator, looking through a patriarchal lens, does not see Emily at all but rather a figment of his own imagination created in conjunction with the cumulative imagination of the town. Like Ellison's invisible man, nobody sees *Emily*. And because nobody sees *her,* she can literally get away with murder. Emily is characterized by her ability to understand and utilize the power that accrues to her from the fact that men do not see her but rather their concept of her: "'I have no taxes in Jefferson. Colonel Sartoris explained it to me.... Tobe!... Show these gentlemen out.'" Relying on the conventional assumptions about ladies who are expected to be neither reasonable nor in touch with reality, Emily presents an impregnable front that vanquishes the men "horse and foot, just as she had vanquished their fathers thirty years before." In spite of their "modern" ideas, this new generation, when faced with Miss Emily, are as much bound by the code of gentlemanly behavior as their fathers were ("They rose when she entered"). This code gives Emily a power that renders the gentlemen unable to function in a situation in which a lady neither sits down herself nor asks them to. They are brought to a "stumbling halt" and can do nothing when confronted with her refusal to engage in rational discourse. Their only recourse in the face of such eccentricity is to engage in behavior unbecoming to gentlemen, and Emily can count on their continuing to see themselves as gentlemen and her as a lady and on their returning a verdict of helpless noninterference.

It is in relation to Emily's disposal of Homer Barron, however, that Faulkner demonstrates most clearly the power of conventional assumptions about the nature of ladies to blind the town to what is going on and to allow Emily to murder with impunity. When Emily buys the poison, it never occurs to anyone that she intends to use it on Homer, so strong is the presumption that ladies when jilted commit suicide, not murder. And when her house begins to smell, the women blame it on the eccentricity of having a man servant rather than a woman, "as if a man – any man – could keep a kitchen properly." And then they hint that her eccentricity may have shaded over into madness, "remembering how old lady Wyatt, her great aunt, had gone completely crazy at last." The presumption of madness, that pre-eminently female response to bereavement, can be used to explain away much in the behavior of ladies whose activities seem a bit odd.

But even more pointed is what happens when the men try not to explain but to do something about the smell: "'Dammit, sir,' Judge Stevens said, 'will you accuse a lady to her face of smelling bad?'" But if a lady cannot be told that she smells, then the cause of the smell cannot be discovered and so her crime is "perfect." Clearly, the assumptions behind the Judge's outraged retort go beyond the myth that ladies are out of touch with reality. His outburst insists that it is the responsibility of gentlemen to make them so. Ladies must not be confronted with facts; they must be shielded from all that is unpleasant. Thus Colonel Sartoris remits Emily's taxes with a palpably absurd story, designed to protect her from an awareness of her poverty and her dependence on charity, and to protect him from having to confront her with it. And thus Judge Stevens will not confront Emily with the fact that her house stinks, though she is living in it and can hardly be unaware of the odor. Committed as they are to the myth that ladies and bad smells cannot coexist, these gentlemen insulate themselves from reality. And by defining a lady as a subhuman and hence sublegal entity, they have created a situation their laws can't touch. They have made it possible for Emily to be extra-legal: "'Why, of course,' the druggist said, 'If that's what you want. But the law requires you to tell what you are going to use it for.' Miss Emily just stared at him, her head tilted back in order to look him eye for eye, until he looked away and went and got the arsenic and wrapped it up." And, finally, they have created a situation in which they become the criminals: "So the next night, after midnight, four men crossed Miss Emily's lawn and slunk about the house like burglars." Above them, "her upright torso motionless as that of an idol," sits Emily, observing them act out their charade of chivalry. As they leave, she confronts them with the reality they are trying to protect her from: she turns on the light so that they may see her watching them. One can only wonder at the fact, and regret, that she didn't call the sheriff and have them arrested for trespassing.

Not only is "A Rose for Emily" a supreme analysis of what men do to women by making them ladies; it is also an exposure of how this act in turn defines and recoils upon men. This is the significance of the dynamic that Faulkner establishes between Emily and Jefferson. And it is equally the point of the dynamic implied between the tableau of Emily and her father and the tableau which greets the men who break down the door of that room in the region above the stairs. When the would-be "suitors" finally get into her father's house, they discover the consequences of his oppression of her, for the violence contained in the rotted corpse of Homer Barron is the mirror image of the violence represented in the tableau, the back-flung front door flung back with a vengeance. Having been consumed by her father, Emily in turn feeds off Homer Barron, becoming, after his death, suspiciously fat. Or, to put it another way, it is as if, after her father's death, she has reversed his act of incorporating her by incorporating and becoming him, metamorphosed from the slender figure in white to the obese figure in black whose hair is "a vigorous iron-gray, like the hair of an active man." She has taken into herself the violence in him which thwarted her and has reenacted it upon Homer Barron.

That final encounter, however, is not simply an image of the reciprocity of violence. Its power of definition also derives from its grotesqueness, which makes finally explicit the grotesqueness that has been latent in the description of Emily throughout the story: "Her skeleton was small and spare; perhaps that was why what would have been merely plumpness in another was obesity in her. She looked bloated, like a body long submerged in motionless water, and of that pallid hue. Her eyes, lost in the fatty ridges of her face, looked like two small pieces of coal pressed into a lump of dough." The impact of this description depends on the contrast it establishes between Emily's reality as a fat, bloated figure in black and the conventional image of a lady – expectations that are fostered in the town by its emblematic memory of Emily as a slender figure in white and in us by the narrator's tone of romantic invocation and by the passage itself. Were she not expected to look so different, were her skeleton not small and spare, Emily would not be so grotesque. Thus, the focus is on the grotesqueness that results when stereotypes are imposed upon reality. And the implication of this focus is that the real grotesque is the stereotype itself. If Emily is both lady and grotesque, then the syllogism must be completed thus: the idea of a lady is grotesque. So Emily is metaphor and mirror for the town of Jefferson; and when, at the end, the town folk finally discover who and what she is, they have in fact encountered who and what they are.

Despite similarities of focus and vision, "A Rose for Emily" is more implicitly feminist than "The Birthmark." For one thing, Faulkner does not have Hawthorne's compulsive ambivalence; one is not invited to misread "A Rose for Emily" as one is invited to misread "The Birthmark." Thus, the interpretation of "The Birthmark" that sees it as a story of misguided idealism, despite its massive oversights, nevertheless *works;* while the efforts to read "A Rose for Emily" as a parable of the relations between North and South, or as a conflict between an old order and a new, or as a story about the human relation to Time, don't work because the attempt to make Emily representative of such concepts stumbles over the fact that woman's condition is not the "human" condition.[2] To understand Emily's experience requires a primary awareness of the fact that she is a woman.

But, more important, Faulkner provides us with an image of retaliation. Unlike Georgiana, Emily does not simply acquiesce; she prefers to murder rather than to die. In this respect she is a welcome change from the image of woman as willing victim that fills the pages of our literature, and whose other face is the ineffective fulminations of Dame Van Winkle. Nevertheless, Emily's action is still reaction. "A Rose for Emily" exposes the poverty of a situation in which turnabout is the only possibility and in which one's acts are neither self-generated nor self-determined but are simply a response to and a reflection of forces outside oneself. Though Emily may be proud, strong, and indomitable, her murder of Homer Barron is finally an indication of the severely limited nature of the power women can wrest from the system that oppresses them. Aylmer's murder of Georgiana is an indication of men's absolute power over women; it is an act performed in the complete security of his ability to legitimize it as a noble and human pursuit. Emily's act has no such context. It is possible only because it can be kept secret; and it can be kept secret only at the cost of exploiting her image as a lady. Furthermore, Aylmer murders Georgiana in order to get rid of her; Emily murders Homer Barron in order to have him.

Patriarchal culture is based to a considerable extent on the argument that men and women are made for each other and on the conviction that "masculinity" and "femininity" are the natural reflection of that divinely ordained complement. Yet, if one reads "The Birthmark" and "A Rose for Emily" as analyses of the consequences of a massive differentiation of everything according to sex, one sees that in reality a sexist culture is one in which men and women are not simply incompatible but murderously so. Aylmer murders Georgiana because he must at any cost get rid of [a] woman; Emily murders Homer Barron because she must at any cost get a man. The two stories define the disparity between cultural myth and cultural reality, and they suggest that in this disparity is the ultimate grotesque.

1 See *Faulkner in the University: Class Conferences at the University of Virginia 1957–1958*, eds. Frederick L. Gwynn and Joseph L. Blotner (Charlottesville, Va.: University of Virginia Press, 1959), pp. 87–88; *Faulkner at Nagano*, ed. Robert A. Jeliffe (Tokyo: Kenkyusha Ltd., 1956), p. 71.

2 For a sense of some of the difficulties involved in reading the story in these terms, I

refer the reader to the collection of criticism edited by M. Thomas Inge, *A Rose for Emily* (Columbus, Oh.: Merrill, 1970).

From Judith Fetterley, *The Resisting Reader. A Feminist Approach to American Fiction.* Bloomington, Ind.: Indiana University Press, 1981, © 1978 by Judith Fetterley.

You will notice that a period of 35–40 years separates the piece by Brooks and Warren from those written by Fetterley and Crosman. This shift in time makes it possible for us to perceive changes in critical "fashion," or reading paradigms. The most obvious difference is that Fetterley and Crosman explicitly focus on the issue of gender, both as it is represented in "A Rose for Emily" and as a factor in the reading experience, while Brooks and Warren do not. In Brooks and Warren's interpretation we can see a New Critical concern with "moral significance" as an important part of the meaning of a literary work. They state their criterion for meaning as follows: "If the story is to be justified, there must be what may be called a moral significance, a meaning in moral terms – not merely psychological terms." As you can see, in Fetterley and Crosman the emphasis on morality has been replaced by other interests. Indeed, Crosman is primarily interested in explaining both the text and his response to it in precisely the "psychological terms" that Brooks and Warren think it is important to transcend.

2. Reread the critical excerpts and identify the assumptions about men's and women's roles that you encounter in them.
3. Since Crosman and Fetterley make a gender position a conscious part of their reading paradigm, and Brooks and Warren do not, what would you say is gained or lost from a) including and b) excluding gender from the reading experience?
4. You will notice that in their first paragraph Brooks and Warren use the word "perhaps" in connection with their attempt to interpret the story, thereby signaling uncertainty or speculation on their part. Look for other evidence of such uncertainty and suggest some possible reasons for their disquiet. Fetterley and Crosman do not explicitly express uncertainty; check, however, whether they downplay or even omit certain aspects of the story as they develop their arguments.

Fetterley's feminist approach shows how gender may be used as a key to "unlock" a dimension of the text not noticed by an earlier generation of critics. You will notice, however, that she focuses on women and femininity, while men and masculinity are of only marginal interest to her. This is a conscious choice on her part.

Indeed, Fetterley explicitly identifies her book as a political act. Like Adrienne Rich, Elaine Showalter, and other feminist critics, she argues that women readers are conditioned to suppress their awareness of their own gender identity when they read literature by men in order that they may appreciate its "universal" values. She argues that in many of the texts by canonical authors of American literature, such as Hemingway and Scott Fitzgerald, these values are in fact misogynist. If women readers are then "taught to think as men, to identify with a male point of view" (a process she calls "the immasculation of women"), they become involved in the "endless division of self against self." In the spirit of the "consciousness-raising" feminism of the 1970s, Fetterley wishes to deploy her critic's role in the cause of empowering women readers by making them aware of the mechanisms of disempowerment hidden in canonical literature. As she puts it herself, "the first act of the feminist critic must be to become a resisting rather than an assenting reader and, by this refusal to assent, to begin the process of exorcizing the male mind that has been implanted in us."

You may have noticed that in "A Rose for Emily" there are a few references to black characters. For instance, Miss Emily has a black servant stay with her until her death; her father, Colonel Sartoris, issues an edict "that no Negro woman should appear on the streets without an apron." The town's black citizens are peripheral in the narrative, and they are all but absent in the critical pieces you have read. In the texts excerpted below, issues of race, racial stereotyping, and racism are central themes. We will look at textual representations of encounters between white (American) and black (African or African-American) characters.

Section Two

In this section we focus on the issue of representing race. You will, no doubt, find the ideological "message" of the excerpts that we ask you to work with quite obvious. The tasks focus primarily on narrative ways of constructing race, and only secondarily on the political and moral reverberations of the textual constructions of race.

EXERCISE 1

In Herman Melville's short story "Benito Cereno," Captain Amasa Delano, an American, boards a ship which seems to him to be in distress. Once on board the *San Dominick*, Captain Delano is met by a crowd of whites and blacks. From the ship's Spanish captain, Benito Cereno, Delano tries to learn the story of the vessel's misadventures. In the three excerpts given below, Captain Delano registers certain scenes on board the *San Dominick*. Read the excerpts and answer the following questions:

Herman Melville: "Benito Cereno"

[1]

'Yes, their owner was quite right in assuring me that no fetters would be needed with his blacks; so that while, as is wont in this transportation, those negroes have always remained upon deck – not thrust below, as in the Guinea-men – they have, also, from the beginning, been freely permitted to range within given bounds at their pleasure.'

Once more the faintness returned – his voice roved – but, recovering, he resumed:

'But it is Babo here to whom, under God, I owe not only my own preservation, but likewise to him, chiefly, the merit is due, of pacifying his more ignorant brethren, when at intervals tempted to murmurings.'

'Ah, master,' sighed the black, bowing his face, 'don't speak of me; Babo is nothing; what Babo has done was but duty.'

'Faithful fellow!' cried Captain Delano. 'Don Benito, envy you such a friend; slave I cannot call him.'

As master and man stood before him, the black upholding the white, Captain Delano could not but bethink him of the beauty of that relationship which could present such a spectacle of fidelity on the one hand and confidence on the other. The scene was heightened by the contrast in dress, denoting their relative positions. The Spaniard wore a loose Chili jacket of dark velvet; white small-clothes and stockings, with silver buckles at the knee and instep; a high-crowned sombrero, of fine grass; a slender sword, silver mounted, hung from a knot in his sash – the last being an almost invariable adjunct, more for utility than ornament, of a South American gentleman's dress to this hour. Excepting when his occasional nervous contortions brought about disarray, there was a certain precision in his attire curiously at variance with the unsightly disorder around; especially in the belittered Ghetto, forward of the mainmast, wholly occupied by the blacks.

The servant wore nothing but wide trowsers, apparently, from their coarseness and patches, made out of some old topsail; they were clean, and confined at the waist by a bit of unstranded rope, which, with his composed, deprecatory air at times, made him look something like a begging friar of St Francis....

[2]

Here the servant, napkin on arm, made a motion as if waiting his master's good pleasure. Don Benito signified his readiness, when, seating him in the Malacca arm-chair, and for the guest's convenience drawing opposite one of the settees, the servant commenced operations by throwing back his master's collar and loosening his cravat.

There is something in the negro which, in a peculiar way, fits him for avocations about one's person. Most negroes are natural valets and hairdressers; taking to the comb and brush congenially as to the castinets, and flourishing them apparently with almost equal satisfaction. There is, too, a smooth tact about them in this employment, with a marvelous, noiseless, gliding briskness, not ungraceful in its way, singularly pleasing to behold, and still more so to be the manipulated subject of. And above all is the great gift of good-humor. Not the mere grin or laugh is here meant. Those were unsuitable. But a certain easy cheerfulness, harmonious in every glance and gesture; as though God had set the whole negro to some pleasant tune.

When to this is added the docility arising from the unaspiring contentment of a limited mind, and that susceptibility of bland attachment sometimes inhering in indisputable inferiors, one readily perceives why those hypochondriacs, Johnson and Byron – it may be, something like the hypochondriac Benito Cereno – took to their hearts, almost to the exclusion of the entire white race, their serving men, the negroes, Barber and Fletcher. But if there be that in the negro which exempts him from the inflicted sourness of the morbid or cynical mind, how, in his most prepossessing aspects, must he appear to a benevolent one? When at ease with respect to exterior things, Captain Delano's nature was not only benign, but familiarly and humorously so. At home, he had often taken rare satisfaction in sitting in his door, watching some free man of color at his work or play. If on a voyage he chanced to have a black sailor, invariably he was on chatty and half-gamesome terms with him. In fact, like most men of a good, blithe heart, Captain Delano took to negroes, not philanthropically, but genially, just as other men to Newfoundland dogs.

Hitherto, the circumstances in which he found the *San Dominick* had repressed the tendency. But in the cuddy, relieved from his former uneasiness, and, for various reasons, more sociably inclined than at any previous period of the day, and seeing the colored servant, napkin on arm, so debonair about his master, in a business so familiar as that of shaving, too, all his old weakness for negroes returned.

Among other things, he was amused with an odd instance of the African love of bright colors and fine shows, in the black's informally taking from the flag-locker a great piece of bunting of all hues, and lavishly tucking it under his master's chin for an apron....

[3]

His attention had been drawn to a slumbering negress, partly disclosed through the lace-work of some rigging, lying, with youthful limbs carelessly disposed, under the lee of the bulwarks, like a doe in the shade of a woodland rock. Sprawling at her lapped breasts, was her wide-awake fawn, stark naked, its black little body half lifted from the deck, crosswise with its dam's; its hands, like two paws, clambering upon her; its mouth and nose ineffectually rooting to get at the mark; and meantime giving a vexatious half-grunt, blending with the composed snore of the negress.

The uncommon vigor of the child at length roused the mother. She started up, at a distance facing Captain Delano. But as if not at all concerned at the attitude in which she had been caught, delightedly she caught the child up, with maternal transports, covering it with kisses.

There's naked nature, now; pure tenderness and love, thought Captain Delano, well pleased.

This incident prompted him to remark the other negresses more particularly than before. He was gratified with their manners: like most uncivilized women, they seemed at once tender of heart and tough of constitution; equally ready to die for their infants or fight for them. Unsophisticated as leopardesses; loving as doves. Ah! thought Captain Delano, these, perhaps, are some of the very women whom Ledyard saw in Africa, and gave such a noble account of.

1. What images are used to describe the Africans? What view of the black race do they imply?
2. What relationships between the white and the black characters are posited in the passages?
3. How would you characterize Captain Delano as an observer in the three scenes?

Toward the end of the story, Captain Delano learns that the slaves, the "one hundred and sixty blacks, of both sexes" on board the *San Dominick*, revolted one night, killed most members of the crew and the passengers (all white), and took over the command of the ship. Babo, the ringleader of the mutiny, planned to sail to Senegal. It was Babo who planned the details of the deception of Captain Delano, threatening to kill Captain Cereno if he did not participate in the playacting. The female slaves participated in the revolt and instigated the male slaves to murder and cruelty.

4. How does the information provided above influence your understanding of Captain Delano and his function in the story?

EXERCISE 2

The following information may further your understanding of the excerpt from Toni Morrison's *Sula*. Helene Wright lives with her husband and her daughter, Nell, in Medallion, Ohio. She was born in New Orleans. Her mother was a Creole prostitute who worked in the Sundown House to which the red shutters mentioned in the excerpt allude. On receiving a letter telling of her grandmother's illness, Helene decides to go to New Orleans.

Read the excerpt below:

Toni Morrison: *Sula*

It was November. November, 1920. Even in Medallion there was a victorious swagger in the legs of white men and a dull-eyed excitement in the eyes of colored veterans.

Helene thought about the trip South with heavy misgiving but decided that she had the best protection: her manner and her bearing, to which she would add a beautiful dress. She bought some deep-brown wool and three-fourths of a yard of matching velvet. Out of this she made herself a heavy but elegant dress with velvet collar and pockets.

Nel watched her mother cutting the pattern from newspapers and moving her eyes rapidly from a magazine model to her own hands. She watched her turn up the kerosene lamp at sunset to sew far into the night.

The day they were ready, Helene cooked a smoked ham, left a note for her lake-bound husband, in case he docked early, and walked head high and arms stiff with luggage ahead of her daughter to the train depot.

It was a longer walk than she remembered, and they saw the train steaming up just as they turned the corner. They ran along the track looking for the coach pointed out to them by the colored porter. Even at that they made a mistake. Helene and her daughter entered a coach peopled by some twenty white men and women. Rather than go back and down the three wooden steps again, Helene decided to spare herself some embarrassment and walk on through to the colored car. She carried two pieces of luggage and a string purse; her daughter carried a covered basket of food.

As they opened the door marked COLORED ONLY, they saw a white conductor coming toward them. It was a chilly day but a light skim of sweat glistened on the woman's face as she and the little girl struggled to hold the door open, hang on to their luggage and enter all at once. The conductor let his eyes travel over the pale yellow woman and then stuck his little finger into his ear, jiggling it free of wax. "What you think you doin', gal?"

Helene looked up at him.

So soon. So soon. She hadn't even begun the trip back. Back to her grandmother's house in the city where the red shutters glowed, and already she had been called "gal." All the old vulnerabilities, all the old fears of being somehow flawed gathered in her stomach and made her hands tremble. She had heard only that one word; it dangled above her wide-brimmed hat, which had slipped, in her exertion, from its carefully leveled placement and was now tilted in a bit of a jaunt over her eye.

Thinking he wanted her tickets, she quickly dropped both the cowhide suitcase and the straw one in order to search for them in her purse. An eagerness to please and an apology for living met in her voice. "I have them. Right here somewhere, sir ..."

The conductor looked at the bit of wax his fingernail had retrieved. "What was you doin' back in there? What was you doin' in that coach yonder?"

Helene licked her lips. "Oh ... I ..." Her glance moved beyond the white man's face to the passengers seated behind him. Four or five black faces were watching, two belonging to soldiers still in their shit-colored uniforms and peaked caps. She saw their closed faces, their locked eyes, and turned for compassion to the gray eyes of the conductor.

"We made a mistake, sir. You see, there wasn't no sign. We just got in the wrong car, that's all. Sir."

"We don't 'low no mistakes on this train. Now git your butt on in there."

He stood there staring at her until she realized that he wanted her to move aside. Pulling Nel by the arm, she pressed herself and her daughter into the foot space in front of a wooden seat. Then, for no earthly reason, at least no reason that anybody could understand, certainly no reason that Nel understood then or later, she smiled. Like a street pup that wags its tail at the very doorjamb of the butcher shop he has been kicked away from only moments before, Helene smiled. Smiled dazzlingly and coquettishly at the salmon-colored face of the conductor.

Nel looked away from the flash of pretty teeth to the other passengers. The two black soldiers, who had been watching the scene with what appeared to be indifference, now looked stricken. Behind Nel was the bright and blazing light of her mother's smile; before her the midnight eyes of the soldiers. She saw the muscles of their faces tighten, a movement under the skin from blood to marble. No change in the expression of the eyes, but a hard wetness that veiled them as they looked at the stretch of her mother's foolish smile.

As the door slammed on the conductor's exit, Helene walked down the aisle to a seat. She looked about for a second to see whether any of the men would help her put the suitcases in the overhead rack. Not a man moved. Helene sat down, fussily, her back toward the men. Nel sat opposite, facing both her mother and the soldiers, neither of whom she could look at. She felt both pleased and ashamed to sense that these men, unlike her father, who worshiped his graceful, beautiful wife, were bubbling with a hatred for her mother that had not been there in the beginning but had been born with the dazzling smile. In the silence that preceded the train's heave, she looked deeply at the folds of her mother's dress. There in the fall of the heavy brown wool she held her eyes. She could not risk letting them travel upward for fear of seeing that the hooks and eyes in the placket of the dress had come undone and exposed the custard-colored skin underneath. She stared at the hem, wanting to believe in its weight but knowing that custard was all that it hid. If this tall, proud woman, this woman who was very particular about her friends, who slipped into church with unequaled elegance, who could quell a roustabout with a look, if *she* were really custard, then there was a chance that Nel was too.

1. What images are used to describe the characters? Compare these images with the ones you identified when analyzing excerpts from Melville's short story. How different or similar are they?
2. From whose perspective is the scene narrated? How does this perspective render the experience of the racial predicament?
3. Two incidents are crucial in the excerpt you have read: the conductor's addressing Helene as "gal" and Helene's smiling. How are these incidents related to race?

EXERCISE 3

1. In the excerpt from *Sula*, the central character is a black woman, just as a black woman is the object of representation in the third excerpt from "Benito Cereno." How different or similar are the positions of the two female black characters? How does gender complicate the representation of race in the texts by Morrison and Melville (excerpt no. 3)?
2. Toni Morrison claims that "until very recently, and regardless of the race of the author, the readers of virtually all of American fiction have been positioned as white" (1992, p. x). Do you find such a positioning in the texts you have analyzed in this unit?
3. William Faulkner and Herman Melville are white male authors; Toni Morrison is an African-American woman writer. To what extent do you think the author's gender and/or racial

identity is important to your reading and understanding of the texts? How important is the knowledge of the historical time and the cultural context of each text to your understanding and evaluation of its representation of race?

In the two texts from which we have selected excerpts, race is not only one of the central themes but it also plays a crucial role in structuring the plot. (For instance, narrative perspective is grounded in certain preconceptions about the white or black race.)

In much of current usage, *race* and *ethnicity* are used interchangeably. A dictionary definition links the concept of race to scientifically "objective" (biological) differences between people:

> **race** (a) any of the major biological divisions of mankind, distinguished by color and texture of hair, color of skin and eyes, stature, bodily proportions, etc.; many ethnologists now consider that there are only three primary divisions, the Caucasian (loosely, white race), Negroid (loosely, *black race*), and Mongoloid (loosely, *yellow race*), each with various subdivisions: the term has acquired so many unscientific connotations that in this sense it is often replaced in scientific usage by *ethnic stock or group*; (b) mankind. (*Webster's New Twentieth Century Dictionary*, 1983 ed.)

Although in contemporary critical theory it is common to speak about the importance of "gender, race, and class" when discussing such issues as, for instance, what it means to be a subject (agent), the concept of ethnicity tends to replace the term race because it is experienced as more neutral than race. *Webster's* defines ethnicity as "ethnic classification or affiliation" and gives the following explanation of the adjective *ethnic:*

> **ethnic** 1. heathen; pagan; pertaining to nations or groups neither Christian nor Jewish. 2. designating or of any of the basic divisions or groups of mankind, as distinguished by customs, characteristics, language, etc.

As you can see from entry 1, the "division" or differences that the definitions of race and ethnicity hinge on are not neutral; they are value-charged. As you have observed in the texts studied, Melville and Morrison make use of the habitual linking of physical appearance (e.g. skin pigmentation or the color and texture of hair) to moral and intellectual characteristics. They also explore the function of physical appearance as a marker of social status. Recent theories dealing with race/ethnicity have shown that in the discourse of the colonizing white Western man, the "Other" – whether an African, an Arab, or a Jew – is most often constructed as savage, lazy, deceitful, irrational, uncivilized, incomprehensible, etc.

Such limited, partial, and stereotyping constructions of ethnic groups – and women – have become the subject of much critical attention in recent years. This has led to a radical questioning of the values informing Western literature, particularly in the United States. Many canonical texts of Western culture have been re-examined for their often racist and sexist representation of women and ethnic groups. These groups, and other "others" have argued for a redressing of the canon dominated by texts written by European white male authors. Such demands have resulted in an introduction into literary courses and anthologies of a number of texts written by women and ethnic writers. Breaking away from the tradition of formalism in literary criticism, a growing number of critics (and teachers) ask "non-literary" (that is, non-aesthetic) questions about literary texts: Is a given text morally, politically, or philosophically "sound"? What ethical and political effects would the teaching of a given text have?

The above-mentioned issues – the representation and reading of race, the revision of the canon, and ethical criticism – are all combined in a statement made by a black member of the staff at the University of Chicago:

> It's hard for me to say this, but I have to say it anyway. I simply can't teach *Huckleberry Finn* again. The way Mark Twain portrays Jim is so offensive to me that I get angry in class, and I can't get all those liberal white kids to understand why I am angry. What's more, I don't think it's right to subject students, black or white, to the many distorted views of race on which that book is based. No, it's not the word "nigger" I'm objecting to, it's the whole range of assumptions about slavery and its consequences, and about how whites should deal with liberated slaves, and how liberated slaves should behave or will behave toward whites, good ones and bad ones. That book is just bad education, and the fact that it's

so cleverly written makes it even more troublesome to me. (Paul Moses, in Booth 1988, p. 3)[1]

WRITTEN ASSIGNMENTS

1. Many canonical stories for girls and boys present the processes involved in the construction of gender and/or racial differences. You may be familiar with such texts as F. H. Burnett's *The Secret Garden*, Louisa May Alcott's *Little Women*, Rudyard Kipling's *The Jungle Book*, or Robert Louis Stevenson's *Treasure Island*. Choose a text that you know well and write a 2–3-page essay on the representation of race or gender in it.

2. As you have noticed while studying the definitions of *race* and *ethnicity* provided in Section Two of this unit, race is defined in terms of "mankind," while ethnic is explained far less neutrally, as meaning "heathen; pagan; pertaining to nations or groups neither Christian nor Jewish." In *Heart of Darkness*, for example, the distinction between Christian (Western) and heathen (African) is crucial for creating the text's meanings. Write a 2–3-page essay reflecting on the applicability of these definitions to any literary text you know well.

See "Feminist and gender studies" and "Ethnic studies" in the Glossary.

---

1 Wayne Booth does not claim to quote his colleague's opinion verbatim. He recalls that Paul Moses made his statement in the 1960s and that it created a "minor scandal" at the university.

Unit Six

Aspects of intertextuality and ideology

In this unit we consider some of the ways in which texts make use of other texts through, for instance, pastiche, quotation, or allusion. We illustrate these techniques with three paintings. We then read the "Friday" texts for their ideological dimensions and reflect on the role of the reader's familiarity with the "parent text" in the process of interpretation.

Material:

> *Section One (paintings)*
> Marcel Duchamp, *Mona Lisa: L.H.O.O.Q* (1919)
> Ferdinand Léger, *Mona Lisa with Keys* (1930)
> René Magritte, *The Gioconda* (1960)
>
> *Section Two (texts)*
> Daniel Defoe, excerpt from *Robinson Crusoe* (1719)
> J. M. Coetzee, excerpt from *Foe* (1986)

Section One: three "Mona Lisa" paintings (see pp. 193–95)

Before you start examining the three reproductions, jot down what associations you have with the name Leonardo da Vinci (1452–1519) and his painting *Mona Lisa* (1503–6). Then look carefully at the reproductions of the three paintings and answer the following questions:

1. Consider the formal composition of the paintings: How does Leonardo da Vinci's portrait of Mona Lisa figure in the three paintings? How has each artist transformed da Vinci's painting? Reflect on your response to the paintings: What emotions and feelings do these transformations stir in you? Which painting do you find most intellectually stimulating?

2. As you certainly know, Leonardo da Vinci's *Mona Lisa* is one of the most valued paintings in our culture, a masterpiece. The painting is often given as an example of a unique artistic expression, and the woman portrayed as an incarnation of eternal femininity. Art historian H. W. Janson mentions the "psychological fascination of the sitter's personality"(p. 440), especially the intriguing smile, as the reason for the painting's fame. He continues: "Clearly, the Mona Lisa embodies a quality of maternal tenderness which was to Leonardo the essence of womanhood. Even the landscape in the background, composed mainly of rocks and water, suggests elemental generative forces" (p. 449). What do you think are Duchamp's, Léger's, and Magritte's attitudes toward the masterpiece?

3. As you may have observed, the Duchamp–Léger–Magritte sequence of Mona Lisa paintings starts with Leonardo da Vinci's painting "fully present." In Léger's version the *Mona Lisa* is "embedded," and in Magritte's most – if not all – of its visual elements disappear (the brown color excepted). What kind of familiarity with the original *Mona Lisa* does each artist presuppose the viewer of his painting to have? How does the gradual disappearance of Leonardo da Vinci's painting affect your interpretive efforts? What is the function of the titles for your understanding of Duchamp's, Léger's, and Magritte's paintings? (You may want to know that the letters L.H.O.O.Q., when read out loud, may be understood as a pun for "Elle a chaud au cul," that is, "She has a hot arse."

Section Two: Daniel Defoe's and J. M. Coetzee's texts

1. Read the excerpts below. As usual, we would like you to note your emotional and intellectual responses to the texts on your first encounter with them.

Daniel Defoe: *Robinson Crusoe*

While I was looking on them, I perceived by my Perspective, two miserable Wretches dragg'd from the Boats, where it seems they were laid by, and were now brought out for the Slaughter. I perceived one of them immediately fell, being knock'd down, I suppose with a Club or Wooden Sword, for that was their way, and two or three others were at work immediately cutting him open for their Cookery, while the other Victim was left standing by himself, till they should be ready for him. In that very Moment this poor Wretch seeing himself a little at Liberty, Nature inspir'd him with Hopes of Life, and he started away from them, and ran with incredible Swiftness along the Sands directly towards me, I mean towards that part of the Coast, where my Habitation was.

I was dreadfully frighted, (that I must acknowledge) when I perceived him to run my Way; and especially, when as I thought I saw him pursued by the whole Body, and now I expected that part of my Dream was coming to pass, and that he would certainly take shelter in my Grove; but I could not depend by any means upon my Dream for the rest of it, (*viz.*) that the other Savages would not pursue him thither, and find him there. However I kept my Station, and my Spirits began to recover, when I found that there was not above three Men that follow'd him, and still more was I encourag'd, when I found that the outstrip'd them exceedingly in running, and gain'd Ground of them, so that if he could but hold it for half an Hour, I saw easily he would fairly get away from them all.

There was between them and my Castle, the Creek which I mention'd often at the first part of my Story, when I landed my Cargoes out of the Ship; and this I saw plainly, he must necessarily swim over, or the poor Wretch would be taken there: But when the Savage escaping came thither, he made nothing of it, tho' the Tide was then up, but plunging in, swam thro' in about Thirty Strokes or thereabouts, landed and ran on with exceeding Strength and Swiftness; when the Three Persons came to the Creek, I found that Two of them could Swim, but the Third cou'd not, and that standing on the other Side, he look'd at the other, but went no further; and soon after went softly back again, which as it happen'd, was very well for him in the main.

I observ'd, that the two who swam, were yet more than twice as long swimming over the Creek, as the Fellow was, that fled from them: It came now very warmly upon my Thoughts, and indeed irresistibly, that now was my Time to get me a Servant, and perhaps a Companion, or Assistant; and that I was call'd plainly by Providence to save this poor Creature's Life; I immediately run down the Ladders with all possible Expedition, fetches my two Guns, for they were both but at the Foot of the Ladders, as I observ'd above; and getting up again, with the same haste, to the Top of the Hill, I cross'd toward the Sea; and having a very short Cut, and all down Hill, clapp'd my self in the way, between the Pursuers, and the Pursu'd; hallowing aloud to him that fled, who looking back, was at first perhaps as much frighted at me, as at them; but I beckon'd with my Hand to him, to come back; and in the mean time, I slowly advanc'd towards the two that follow'd; then rushing at once upon the foremost, I knock'd him down with the Stock of my Piece; I was loath to fire, because I would not have the rest hear; though at that distance, it would not have been easily heard, and being out of Sight of the Smoke too, they wou'd not have easily known what to make of it: Having knock'd this Fellow down, the other who pursu'd with him stopp'd, as if he had been frighted; and I advanc'd a-pace towards him; but as I came nearer, I perceiv'd presently, he had a Bow and Arrow, and was fitting it to shoot at me; so I was then necessitated to shoot at him first, which I did, and kill'd him at the first Shoot; the poor Savage who fled, but had stopp'd; though he saw both his Enemies fallen, and kill'd, as he thought; yet was so frighted with the Fire, and Noise of my Piece, that he stood Stock still, and neither came forward or went backward, tho' he seem'd rather enclin'd to fly still, than to come on; I hollow'd again to him, and made Signs to come forward, which he easily understood, and came a little way, then stopp'd again, and then a little further, and stopp'd again, and I cou'd then perceive that he stood trembling, as if he had been taken Prisoner, and had just been to be kill'd, as his two Enemies were; I beckon'd him again to come to me, and gave him all the Signs of Encouragement that I could think of, and he came nearer and nearer, kneeling down every Ten or Twelve steps in token of acknowledgement for my saving his Life: I smil'd at him, and look'd pleasantly, and beckon'd to him to come still nearer; at length he came close to me, and then he kneel'd down again, kiss'd the Ground, and laid his Head upon the Ground, and taking me by the Foot, set my Foot upon his Head; this it seems was in token of swearing to be my Slave for ever; I took him up, and made much of him, and encourag'd him all I could. But there was more work to do yet, for I perceiv'd the Savage who I knock'd down, was not kill'd, but stunn'd with the blow, and began to come to himself; so I pointed to him, and showing him the Savage, that he was not dead; upon this he spoke some Words to me, and though I could not understand them, yet I thought they were pleasant to hear, for they were the first sound of a Man's Voice, that I had heard, *my own excepted,* for above Twenty Five Years. But there was no time for such Reflections now, the Savage who was knock'd down recover'd himself so far, as to sit up upon the Ground, and I perceived that my Savage began to be afraid; but when I saw that, I presented my other Piece at the Man, as if I would shoot him, upon this my Savage, *for so I call him now,* made a Motion to me to lend him my Sword, which hung naked in a Belt by my side; so I did: he no sooner had it, but he runs to his Enemy, and at one blow cut off his Head as cleaverly, no Executioner in *Germany,* could have done it sooner or better; which I thought very strange, for one who I had Reason to believe never saw a Sword in his Life before, except their own Wooden Swords; however it seems, as I learn'd afterwards, they make their Wooden Swords so sharp, so heavy, and the Wood is so hard, that they will cut off Heads even with them, ay and Arms, and that at one blow too; when he had done this, he comes laughing to me in Sign of Triumph, and brought me the Sword again, and with abundance of Gestures which I did not understand, laid it down with the Head of the Savage, that he had kill'd just before me.

But that which astonish'd him most, was to know how I had kill'd the other Indian so far off, so pointing to him, he made Signs to me to let him go to him, so I bad ham go, as well as I could, when he came to him, he stood like one amaz'd, looking at him, turn'd him first on one side, then on t'other, look'd at the Wound the Bullet had made, which it seems was just in his Breast, where it had made a Hole, and no great Quantity of Blood had follow'd, but he had bled inwardly, for he was quite dead; He took up his Bow, and Arrows, and came back, so I turn'd to go away, and beckon'd to him to follow me, making Signs to him, that more might come after them.

Upon this he sign'd to me, that he should bury them with Sand, that they might not be seen by the rest if they follow'd; and so I made Signs again to him to do so; he fell to Work, and in an instant he had scrap'd a Hole in the Sand, with his Hands, big enough to bury the first in, and then dragg'd him into it, and cover'd him, and did so also by the other; I believe he had bury'd them both in a Quarter of an Hour; then calling him away, I carry'd him not to my Castle, but quite away to my Cave, on the farther Part of the Island; so I did not let my Dream come to pass in that Part, *viz.* That he came into my Grove for shelter.

Here I gave him Bread, and a Bunch of Raisins to eat, and a Draught of Water, which I found he was indeed in great Distress for, by his Running; and having refresh'd him, I made Signs for him to go lie down and sleep; pointing to a Place where I had laid a great Parcel of Rice Straw, and a Blanket upon it, which I used to sleep upon my self sometimes; so the poor Creature laid down, and went to sleep.

He was a comely handsome Fellow, perfectly well made; with straight strong Limbs, not too large; tall and well shap'd, and as I reckon, about twenty six Years of Age. He had a very good Countenance, not a fierce and surly Aspect; but seem'd to have something very manly in his Face, and yet he had all the Sweetness and Softness of an *European* in his Countenance too, especially when he smil'd. His Hair was long and black, not curl'd like Wool; his Forehead very high, and large, and a great Vivacity and sparkling Sharpness in his Eyes. The Colour of his Skin was not quite black, but very tawny; and yet not of an ugly yellow nauseous tawny, as the *Brasilians,* and *Virginians,* and other Natives of *America* are; but of a bright kind of a dun olive Colour, that had in it something very agreeable; tho' not very easy to describe. His Face was round, and plump; his Nose small, not flat like the Negroes, a very good Mouth, thin Lips, and his fine Teeth well set, and white as Ivory. After he had slumber'd, rather than slept, about half an Hour, he wak'd again, and comes out of the Cave to me; for I had been milking my Goats, which I had in the Enclosure just by: When he espy'd me, he came running to me, laying himself down again upon the Ground, with all the possible Signs of an humble thankful Disposition, making a many antick Gestures to show it: At last he lays his Head flat upon the Ground, close to my Foot, and sets my other Foot upon his Head, as he had done before; and after this, made all the Signs to me of Subjection, Servitude, and Submission imaginable, to let me know, how he would serve me as long as he liv'd; I understood him in many Things, and let him know, I was very well pleas'd with him; in a little Time I began to speak to him, and teach him to speak to me; and first, I made him know his Name should be *Friday,* which was the Day I sav'd his Life; I call'd him so for the Memory of the Time; I likewise taught him to say *Master,* and then let him know, that was to be my Name; I likewise taught him to say, YES, and NO, and to know the Meaning of them; I gave him some Milk, in an earthen Pot, and let him see me Drink it before him, and sop my Bread in it; and I gave him a Cake of Bread, to do the like, which he quickly comply'd with, and made Signs that it was very good for him.

J. M. Coetzee: *Foe*

'At last I could row no further. My hands were blistered, my back was burned, my body ached. With a sigh, making barely a splash, I slipped overboard. With slow strokes, my long hair floating about me, like a flower of the sea, like an anemone, like a jellyfish of the kind you see in the waters of Brazil, I swam towards the strange island, for a while swimming as I had rowed, against the current, then all at once free of its grip, carried by the waves into the bay and on to the beach.

'There I lay sprawled on the hot sand, my head filled with the orange blaze of the sun, my petticoat (which was all I had escaped with) baking dry upon me, tired, grateful, like all the saved.

'A dark shadow fell upon me, not of a cloud but of a man with a dazzling halo about him. "Castaway," I said with my thick dry tongue. "I am cast away. I am all alone." And I held out my sore hands.

'The man squatted down beside me. He was black: a Negro with a head of fuzzy wool, naked save for a pair of rough drawers. I lifted myself and studied the flat face, the small dull eyes, the broad nose, the thick lips, the skin not black but a dark grey, dry as if coated with dust. "*Agua,*" I said, trying Portuguese, and made a sign of drinking. He gave no reply, but regarded me as he would a seal or a porpoise thrown up by the waves, that would shortly expire and might then be cut up for food. At his side he had a spear. I have come to the wrong island, I thought, and let my head sink: I have come to an island of cannibals.

'He reached out and with the back of his hand touched my arm. He is trying my flesh, I thought. But by and by my breathing slowed and I grew calmer. He smelled of fish, and of sheepswool on a hot day.

'Then, since we could not stay thus forever, I sat up and again began to make motions of drinking. I had rowed all morning, I had not drunk since the night before, I no longer cared if he killed me afterwards so long as I had water.

'The Negro rose and signed me to follow. He led me, stiff and sore, across sand-dunes and along a path ascending to the hilly interior of the island. But we had scarcely begun to climb when I felt a sharp hurt, and drew from my heel a long black-tipped thorn. Though I chafed it, the heel quickly swelled till I could not so much as hobble for the pain. The Negro offered me his back, indicating he would carry me. I hesitated to accept, for he was a slight fellow, shorter than I. But there was no help for it. So part-way skipping on one leg, part-way riding on his back, with my petticoat gathered up and my chin brushing his springy hair, I ascended the hillside, my fear of him abating in this strange backwards embrace. He took no heed where he set his feet, I noted, but crushed under his soles whole clusters of the thorns that had pierced my skin.

'For readers reared on travellers' tales, the words *desert isle* may conjure up a place of soft sands and shady trees where brooks run to quench the castaway's thirst and ripe fruit falls into his hand, where no more is asked of him than to drowse the days away till a ship calls to fetch him home. But the island on which I was cast away was quite another place: a great rocky hill with a flat top, rising sharply from the sea on all sides except one, dotted with drab bushes that never flowered and never shed their leaves. Off the island grew beds of brown seaweed which, borne ashore by the waves, gave off a noisome stench and supported swarms of large pale fleas. There were ants scurrying everywhere, of the same kind we had in Bahia, and another pest, too, living in the dunes: a tiny insect that hid between your toes and ate its way into the flesh. Even Friday's hard skin was not proof against it: there were bleeding cracks in his feet, though he paid them no heed. I saw no snakes, but lizards came out in the heat of the day to sun themselves, some small and agile, others large and clumsy, with blue ruffs about their gills which they would flare out when alarmed, and hiss, and glare. I caught one of them in a bag and tried to tame it, feeding it flies; but it would not take dead meat, so at last I set it free. Also there were apes (of whom I will say more later) and birds, birds everywhere: not only flocks of sparrows (or so I called them) that flitted all day chirruping from bush to bush, but on the cliffs above the sea great tribes of gulls and mews and gannets and cormorants, so that the rocks were white with their droppings. And in the sea porpoises and seals and fish of all kinds. So if the company of brutes had been enough for me, I might have lived most happily on my island. But who, accustomed to the fullness of human speech, can be content with caws and chirps and screeches, and the barking of seals, and the moan of the wind?

'At last we came to the end of our climb and my porter halted to catch his breath. I found myself on a level plateau not far from some kind of encampment. On all sides stretched the shimmering sea, while to the east the ship that had brought me receded under full sail.

'My one thought was for water. I did not care to what fate I was being borne so long as I could drink. At the gate of the encampment stood a man, dark-skinned and heavily bearded. "*Agua,*" I said, making signs. He gestured to the Negro, and I saw I was talking to a European. "*Fala inglez?*" I asked, as I had learned to say in Brazil. He nodded. The Negro brought me a bowl of water. I drank, and he brought more. It was the best water I ever had.

'The stranger's eyes were green, his hair burnt to a straw colour. I judged he was sixty years of age. He wore (let me give my description of him all together) a jerkin, and drawers to below his knees, such as we see watermen wear on the Thames, and a tall cap rising in a cone, all of these made of pelts laced together, the fur outwards, and a stout pair of sandals. In his belt were a short stick and a knife. A mutineer, was my first thought: yet another mutineer, set ashore by a merciful captain, with one of the Negroes of the island, whom he has made his servant. "My name is Susan Barton," I said. "I was cast adrift by the crew of the ship yonder. They killed their master and did this to me." And all at once, though I had remained dry-eyed through all the insults done me on board ship and through the hours of despair when I was alone on the waves with the captain lying dead at my feet, a handspike jutting from his eye-socket, I fell to crying. I sat on the bare earth with my sore foot between my hands and rocked back and forth and sobbed like a child, while the stranger (who was of course the Cruso I told you of) gazed at me more as if I were a fish cast up by the waves than an unfortunate fellow-creature.

From J. M. Coetzee, *Foe*. London: Martin Secker & Warburg Ltd, 1987. Reprinted by permission.

2. Now examine each text carefully in order to answer the following questions:
   a. How is the narrator in each text positioned in relation to the other character? Consider here the positioning of the two characters in space, in relation to danger, in terms of help offered or needed, as regards knowledge, etc.
   b. How is the physical appearance of Friday described? What features are mentioned, what adjectives and descriptive phrases are used, and what is their emotional value?
   c. How do the narrator and the other characters communicate?
   d. Whose feelings are presented in the texts? What are they? From what perspective are they presented?
   e. How is the moment of physical contact between the characters presented in each text?
3. Reflect now on the possible meanings of your textual observations. What "message" can the reader "find" in the text if he/she identifies with Crusoe? if he/she inhabits the position of Friday?

if the reader reads from the position of a woman? Articulations of beliefs concerning the issues of race, gender, and knowledge, informing the construction of the fictional world, are the most explicit signals of an ideology. What ideology does Defoe's text articulate? How does it compare with the ideology articulated in Coetzee's novel?

4. Taking into account what you consider to be crucial similarities as well as differences between the texts, reflect on how Defoe's novel, being the "original," affects your understanding of Coetzee's text.

In history of literature courses you may have learned that in many epochs the imitation of model (canonical) texts was considered a most praiseworthy mode of artistic expression. Many writers, for instance, sought and acknowledged the influence of great classical works. One example is Milton, who in *Paradise Lost* pays tribute to Dante, who in turn, in *La divina commedia*, acknowledges his debt to Virgil. Establishing acknowledged as well as unacknowledged affiliations between texts has been one of the interests of historical scholarship. In the study of influence, biography has always been an important source of information about the author's intention and his/her familiarity with a given text/author.

Recent literary theory tends to question the concept of "influence" because it implies the possibility of both the "uniqueness" and the "originality" of a work (when no influence of prior texts can be detected) *and* a clear-cut affiliation between works and authors. Rather than seeking Ur-texts or "sources" and discussing derivation, much contemporary criticism focuses on the *intertextual* aspects of texts, shifting our attention from the work, its place in the canon, and its author's relation to the work to the reader's acts of making sense of the text through his/her knowledge of other texts. Each utterance (text) is seen as caught up in a context of other utterances (texts); the meaning of each sign is informed by the many, often conflicting, ways in which it has been used by speakers throughout history.

We find it helpful to think about intertextuality along the lines suggested by Michel Foucault: "The frontiers of a book are never clear-cut: beyond the title, the first lines, and the last full-stop, beyond its internal configuration and its autonomous form, it is caught up in a system of references to other books, other texts, other sentences: it is a node within a network" (quoted in Hutcheon, p. 127).

In this unit we have examined a few special cases of intertextuality, namely indisputably conscious appropriations of two canonical texts, the Mona Lisa painting and Defoe's novel, by twentieth-century artists. We selected the paintings to illustrate three types of intertextuality: pastiche (a deliberate use of the work of another artist in a more or less unchanged form), quotation (the technique of inserting or embedding parts of an earlier text into a new one), and allusion (an implied reference to another work of art). In selecting Defoe's text we wanted to focus attention not only on how one text is present within another, but also on how the new text (implicitly and explicitly) comments on the parent text's ideology and its cultural inscription. In both cases, we are faced with overtly parodic intertextuality.

This overtly parodic intertextuality is often employed in the service of a critique of the ideology of the "original" text. In his rewriting of the classic eighteenth-century text from the perspective of the concerns of the late twentieth century, Coetzee focuses on some of the ideological subtexts of Defoe's novel. He examines certain myths, assumptions, and beliefs which were current in the early eighteenth-century English culture and which inform *Robinson Crusoe*. One of these myths is the belief in the "natural" superiority of the white man; another is the representation of the middle-class white man as industrious, thrifty, and hard-working. Coetzee also makes visible – and plays with – the conventions of the "desert island" narrative by, for instance, inserting a woman into the "typically male" setting of the island.

WRITTEN ASSIGNMENTS

1. Discuss the effects of Coetzee's introduction of a woman into the classic male "desert island" narrative.
2. Write an essay analyzing Daniel Spoerri's "quotation" of *Mona Lisa* in *Using a Rembrandt as an Ironing Board* (1964). (See p. 196.)

See "Text," "Ideology," and "Intertextuality" in the Glossary.

Unit Seven

Aspects of narrative in fiction and film

The aim of this unit is to introduce you to certain concepts which are used in the study of narrative and which are generally applied in the analysis of prose fiction. These concepts are used when discussing the ways in which meaning is produced. Then we turn to film versions of the two novels in order to examine how a literary text can be presented in a medium which has a different narrative form.

Material:

> F. Scott Fitzgerald, opening pages from *The Great Gatsby* (1925)
> *The Great Gatsby* (1974), opening scenes from Jack Clayton's film (screenplay by Francis Ford Coppola)
> John Fowles, opening pages from *The French Lieutenant's Woman* (1969)
> *The French Lieutenant's Woman* (1981), opening scenes from Karel Reisz's film (screenplay by Harold Pinter)

It is likely that you are already familiar with the basic dynamics of the communication taking place in a narrative: a narrator (a teller) tells a narratee (an addressee or listener) a story (a sequence of events which are somehow connected). Apart from this narrative communication (which takes place within the text), theorists sometimes speak about the communication which takes place between an implied author and an implied reader.[1] The categories of the implied author and the implied reader are *constructs* of the actual author and the actual reader. The characteristics of both the implied author and the implied reader are implicit in the text in such elements as the genre conventions, the choice of language register, and references to other texts. The categories of the implied author and reader are useful in distinguishing between what may be called the "image" of the author and reader as it emerges from a given text and the real, flesh-and-blood author and reader. These different categories of tellers and listeners and the communicative acts in which they participate are presented in the following diagram:[2]

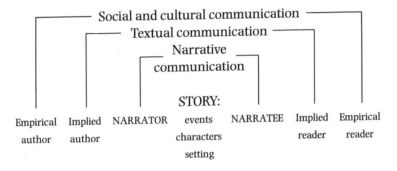

		Social and cultural communication					
			Textual communication				
				Narrative communication			
			STORY:				
Empirical author	Implied author	NARRATOR	events characters setting	NARRATEE	Implied reader	Empirical reader

The focus of this unit will be on the level of narrative communication. Below we briefly present a few of the analytical concepts that are used when discussing fictional narratives. These categories, you should remember, are abstractions, and their usefulness and limitations become clearer during the actual work of analyzing

1 If you would like to learn more about these categories, you may begin by consulting two seminal books. Wayne Booth's *The Rhetoric of Fiction* discusses the notion of the implied author. Wolfgang Iser's *The Implied Reader: Patterns of Communication in Prose Fiction from Bunyan to Beckett* studies how the text structures the potential meaning by steering the reading process.
2 We follow Shlomith Rimmon-Kenan's suggestions put forward in *Narrative Fiction: Contemporary Poetics* in our presentation of the basic components of the narrative. Since she illustrates the concepts with references to a number of literary texts, you may want to consult her book for further clarification.

narratives. After each presentation we ask you to look at the excerpts from the two novels in the light of a specific narrative component. We would like to stress that the aim of the tasks is not to elicit clear-cut "correct" answers (there are a number of possible ones), but rather to initiate you into a process of thinking about narrative in terms of its semantic components or "building blocks."

In this unit we ask you to work with excerpts. Admittedly, this is not an ideal situation. Literary analysis is normally conducted with the knowledge of the narrative's complete plot. Yet even when critics discuss the whole text, there may be considerable disagreement among them regarding, for instance, what constitutes the inciting moment or what is to be regarded as a flashback. Bearing this in mind, try to reflect on why you choose a certain textual element rather than on whether your choice is "correct."

F. Scott Fitzgerald: *The Great Gatsby*
Chapter 1

In my younger and more vulnerable years my father gave me some advice that I've been turning over in my mind ever since.

'Whenever you feel like criticising anyone,' he told me, 'just remember that all the people in this world haven't had the advantages that you've had.'

He didn't say any more, but we've always been unusually communicative in a reserved way, and I understood that he meant a great deal more than that. In consequence, I'm inclined to reserve all judgments, a habit that has opened up many curious natures to me and also made me the victim of not a few veteran bores. The abnormal mind is quick to detect and attach itself to this quality when it appears in a normal person, and so it came about that in college I was unjustly accused of being a politician, because I was privy to the secret griefs of wild, unknown men. Most of the confidences were unsought – frequently I have feigned sleep, preoccupation, or a hostile levity when I realized by some unmistakable sign that an intimate revelation was quivering on the horizon; for the intimate revelations of young men, or at least the terms in which they express them, are usually plagiaristic and marred by obvious suppressions. Reserving judgments is a matter of infinite hope. I am still a little afraid of missing something if I forget that, as my father snobbishly suggested, and I snobbishly repeat, a sense of the fundamental decencies is parcelled out unequally at birth.

And, after boasting this way of my tolerance, I come to the admission that it has a limit. Conduct may be founded on the hard rock or the wet marshes, but after a certain point I don't care what it's founded on. When I came back from the East last autumn I felt that I wanted the world to be in uniform and at a sort of moral attention forever; I wanted no more riotous excursions with privileged glimpses into the human heart. Only Gatsby, the man who gives his name to this book, was exempt from my reaction – Gatsby, who represented everything for which I have an unaffected scorn. If personality is an unbroken series of successful gestures, then there was something gorgeous about him, some heightened sensitivity to the promises of life, as if he were related to one of those intricate machines that register earthquakes ten thousand miles away. This responsiveness had nothing to do with that flabby impressionability which is dignified under the name of the 'creative temperament' – it was an extraordinary gift for hope, a romantic readiness such as I have never found in any other person and which it is not likely I shall ever find again. No – Gatsby turned out all right at the end; it is what preyed on Gatsby, what foul dust floated in the wake of his dreams that temporarily closed out my interest in the abortive sorrows and shortwinded elations of men.

*

My family have been prominent, well-to-do people in this Middle Western city for three generations. The Carraways are something of a clan, and we have a tradition that we're descended from the Dukes of Buccleuch, but the actual founder of my line was my grandfather's brother, who came here in fifty-one, sent a substitute to the Civil War, and started the wholesale hardware business that my father carries on to-day.

I never saw this great-uncle, but I'm supposed to look like him – with special reference to the rather hard-boiled painting that hangs in father's office. I graduated from New Haven in 1915, just a quarter of a century after my father, and a little later I participated in that delayed Teutonic migration know as the Great War. I enjoyed the counter-raid so thoroughly that I came back restless. Instead of being the warm centre of the world, the Middle West now seemed like the ragged edge of the universe – so I decided to go East and learn the bond business. Everybody I knew was in the bond business, so I supposed it could support one more single man. All my aunts and uncles talked it over as if they were choosing a prep school for me, and finally said, 'Why – ye-es,' with very grave, hesitant faces. Father agreed to finance me for a year, and after various delays I came East, permanently, I thought, in the spring of twenty-two.

The practical thing was to find rooms in the city, but it was a warm season, and I had just left a country of wide lawns and friendly trees, so when a young man at the office suggested that we take a house together in a commuting town, it sounded like a great idea. He found the house, a weather-beaten cardboard bungalow at eighty a month, but at the last minute the firm ordered him to Washington, and I went out to the country alone. I had a dog – at least I had him for a few days until he ran away – and an old Dodge and a Finnish woman, who made my bed and cooked breakfast and muttered Finnish wisdom to herself over the electric stove.

It was lonely for a day or so until one morning some man, more recently arrived than I, stopped me on the road.

'How do you get to West Egg village?' he asked helplessly.

I told him. And as I walked on I was lonely no longer. I was a guide, a pathfinder, an original settler. He had casually conferred on me the freedom of the neighbourhood.

And so with the sunshine and the great bursts of leaves growing on the trees, just as things grow in fast movies, I had that familiar conviction that life was beginning over again with the summer.

There was so much to read, for one thing, and so much fine health to be pulled down out of the young breath-giving air. I bought a dozen volumes on banking and credit and investment securities, and they stood on my shelf in red and gold like new money from the mint, promising to unfold the shining secrets that only Midas and Morgan and Maecenas knew. And I had the high intention of reading many other books besides. I was rather literary in college – one year I wrote a series of very solemn and obvious editorials for the Yale News – and now I was going to bring back all such things into my life and become again that most limited of all specialists, the 'well-rounded man.' This isn't just an epigram – life is much more successfully looked at from a single window, after all.

It was a matter of chance that I should have rented a house in one of the strangest communities in North America. It was on that slender riotous island which extends itself due east of New York – and where there are, among other natural curiosities, two unusual formations of land. Twenty miles from the city a pair of enormous eggs, identical in contour and separated only by a courtesy bay, jut out into the most domesticated body of salt water in the Western hemisphere, the great wet barnyard of Long Island Sound. They are not perfect ovals – like the egg in the Columbus story, they are both crushed flat at the contact end – but their physical resemblance must be a source of perpetual wonder to the gulls that fly overhead. To the wingless a more interesting phenomenon is their dissimilarity in every particular except shape and size.

I lived at West Egg, the – well, the less fashionable of the two, though this is a most superficial tag to express the bizarre and not a little sinister contrast between them. My house was at the very tip of the egg, only fifty yards from the Sound, and squeezed between two huge places that rented for twelve or fifteen thousand a season. The one on my right was a colossal affair by any standard – it was a factual imitation of some Hôtel de Ville in Normandy, with a tower on one side, spanking new under a thin beard of raw ivy, and a marble swimming pool, and more than forty acres of lawn and garden. It was Gatsby's mansion. Or, rather, as I didn't know Mr Gatsby, it was a mansion inhabited by a gentleman of that name. My own house was an eyesore, but it was a small eyesore, and it had been over-looked, so I had a view of the water, a partial view of my neighbour's lawn, and the consoling proximity of millionaires – all for eighty dollars a month.

Across the courtesy bay the white palaces of fashionable East Egg glit-tered along the water, and the history of the summer really begins on the evening I drove over there to have dinner with the Tom Buchanans. Daisy was my second cousin once removed, and I'd known Tom in college. And just after the war I spent two days with them in Chicago.

Her husband, among various physical accomplishments, had been one of the most powerful ends that ever played football at New Haven – a national figure in a way, one of those men who reach such an acute limited excel-lence at twenty-one that everything afterward savours of anti-climax. His family were enormously wealthy – even in college his freedom with money was a matter for reproach – but now he'd left Chicago and come East in a fashion that rather took your breath away: for instance, he'd brought down a string of polo ponies from Lake Forest. It was hard to realize that a man in my own generation was wealthy enough to do that.

Why they came East I don't know. They had spent a year in France for no particular reason, and then drifted here and there unrestfully wherever people played polo and were rich together. This was a permanent move, said Daisy over the telephone, but I didn't believe it – I had no sight into Daisy's heart, but I felt that Tom would drift on forever seeking, a little wistfully, for the dramatic turbulence of some irrecoverable football game.

And so it happened that on a warm windy evening I drove over to East Egg to see two old friends whom I scarcely knew at all. Their house was even more elaborate than I expected, a cheerful red-and-white Georgian Colonial mansion, overlooking the bay. The lawn started at the beach and ran toward the front door for a quarter of a mile, jumping over sun-dials and brick walls and burning gardens – finally when it reached the house drifting up the side in bright vines as though from the momentum of its run. The front was broken by a line of french windows, glowing now with reflected gold and wide open to the warm windy afternoon, and Tom Buchanan in riding clothes was standing with his legs apart on the front porch.

He had changed since his New Haven years. Now he was a sturdy straw-haired man of thirty with a rather hard mouth and a supercilious manner. Two shining arrogant eyes had established dominance over his face and gave him the appearance of always leaning aggressively forward. Not even the effeminate swank of his riding clothes could hide the enormous power of that body – he seemed to fill those glistening boots until he strained the top lacing, and you could see a great pack of muscle shifting when his shoulders moved under his thin coat. It was a body capable of enormous leverage – a cruel body.

His speaking voice, a gruff husky tenor, added to the impression of fractiousness he conveyed. There was a touch of paternal contempt in it, even toward people he liked – and there were men at New Haven who had hated his guts.

'Now, don't think my opinion on these matters is final,' he seemed to say, 'just because I'm stronger and more of a man than you are.' We were in the same senior society, and while we were never intimate I always had the impression that he approved of me and wanted me to like him with some harsh, defiant wistfulness of his own.

We talked for a few minutes on the sunny porch.

'I've got a nice place here,' he said, his eyes flashing about restlessly.

Turning me around by one arm, he moved a broad flat hand along the front vista, including in its sweep a sunken Italian garden, a half acre of deep, pungent roses, and a snub-nosed motor-boat that bumped the tide offshore.

'It belonged to Demaine, the oil man.' He turned me around again, politely and abruptly. 'We'll go inside.'

We walked through a high hallway into a bright rosy-coloured space, fragilely bound into the house by french windows at either end. The windows were ajar and gleaming white against the fresh grass outside that seemed to grow a little way into the house. A breeze blew through the room, blew curtains in at one end and out the other like pale flags, twisting them up toward the frosted wedding-cake of the ceiling, and then rippled over the wine-coloured rug, making a shadow on it as wind does on the sea.

The only completely stationary object in the room was an enormous

couch on which two young women were buoyed up as though upon an anchored balloon. They were both in white, and their dresses were rippling
and fluttering as if they had just been blown back in after a short flight
around the house. I must have stood for a few moments listening to the
whip and snap of the curtains and the groan of a picture on the wall. Then
there was a boom as Tom Buchanan shut the rear windows and the caught
wind died out about the room, and the curtains and the rugs and the two
young women ballooned slowly to the floor.

The younger of the two was a stranger to me. She was extended full
length at her end of the divan, completely motionless, and with her chin
raised a little, as if she were balancing something on it which was quite
likely to fall. If she saw me out of the corner of her eyes she gave no hint of
it – indeed, I was almost surprised into murmuring an apology for having
disturbed her by coming in.

The other girl, Daisy, made an attempt to rise – she leaned slightly forward with a conscientious expression – then she laughed, an absurd, charming little laugh, and I laughed too and came forward into the room.

'I'm p-paralyzed with happiness.'

She laughed again, as if she said something very witty, and held my
hand for a moment, looking up into my face, promising that there was no
one in the world she so much wanted to see. That was a way she had. She
hinted in a murmur that the surname of the balancing girl was Baker. (I've
heard it said that Daisy's murmur was only to make people lean toward her;
an irrelevant criticism that made it no less charming.)

At any rate, Miss Baker's lips fluttered, she nodded at me almost imper-
ceptibly, and then quickly tipped her head back again – the object she was
balancing had obviously tottered a little and given her something of a
fright. Again a sort of apology arose to my lips. Almost any exhibition of
complete self-sufficiency draws a stunned tribute from me.

I looked back at my cousin, who began to ask me questions in her low,
thrilling voice. It was the kind of voice that the ear follows up and down, as
if each speech is an arrangement of notes that will never be played again.
Her face was sad and lovely with bright things in it, bright eyes and a bright
passionate mouth, but there was an excitement in her voice that men who
had cared for her found difficult to forget: a singing compulsion, a whispered 'Listen,' a promise that she had done gay, exciting things just a while
since and that there were gay, exciting things hovering in the next hour.

I told her how I had stopped off in Chicago for a day on my way East, and how a dozen people had sent their love through me.

'Do they miss me?' she cried ecstatically.

'The whole town is desolate. All the cars have the left rear wheel painted black as a mourning wreath, and there's a persistent wail all night along the north shore.'

'How gorgeous! Let's go back, Tom. To-morrow!'

John Fowles: *The French Lieutenant's Woman*
Chapter 1

> Stretching eyes west
> Over the sea,
> Wind foul or fair,
> Always stood she
> Prospect-impressed;
> Solely out there
> Did her gaze rest,
> Never elsewhere
> Seemed charm to be.
>   HARDY, 'The Riddle'

An easterly is the most disagreeable wind in Lyme Bay – Lyme Bay being that largest bite from the underside of England's outstretched south-western leg – and a person of curiosity could at once have deduced several strong probabilities about the pair who began to walk down the quay at Lyme Regis, the small but ancient eponym of the inbite, one incisively sharp and blustery morning in the late March of 1867.

The Cobb has invited what familiarity breeds for at least seven hundred years, and the real Lymers will never see much more to it than a long claw of old grey wall that flexes itself against the sea. In fact, since it lies well apart from the main town, a tiny Piraeus to a microscopic Athens, they seem almost to turn their backs on it. Certainly it has cost them enough in repairs through the centuries to justify a certain resentment. But to a less tax-paying, or more discriminating, eye it is quite simply the most beautiful sea-rampart on the south coast of England. And not only because it is, as the guide-books say, redolent of seven hundred years of English history, because ships sailed to meet the Armada from it, because Monmouth landed beside it ... but finally because it is a superb fragment of folk-art.

Primitive yet complex, elephantine but delicate; as full of subtle curves and volumes as a Henry Moore or a Michelangelo; and pure, clean, salt, a paragon of mass. I exaggerate? Perhaps, but I can be put to the test, for the Cobb has changed very little since the year of which I write; though the town of Lyme has, and the test is not fair if you look back towards land.

However, if you had turned northward and landward in 1867, as the man that day did, your prospect would have been harmonious. A picturesque congeries of some dozen or so houses and a small boatyard – in which, arklike on its stocks, sat the thorax of a lugger – huddled at where the Cobb runs back to land. Half a mile to the east lay, across sloping meadows, the thatched and slated roofs of Lyme itself; a town that had its heyday in the Middle Ages and has been declining ever since. To the west sombre grey cliffs, known locally as Ware Cleeves, rose steeply from the shingled beach where Monmouth entered upon his idiocy. Above them and beyond, stepped massively inland, climbed further cliffs masked by dense woods. It is in this aspect that the Cobb seems most a last bulwark – against all that wild eroding coast to the west. There too I can be put to proof. No house lay visible then or, beyond a brief misery of beach-huts, lies today in that direction.

The local spy – and there was one – might thus have deduced that these two were strangers, people of some taste, and not to be denied their enjoyment of the Cobb by a mere harsh wind. On the other hand he might, focusing his telescope more closely, have suspected that a mutual solitude interested them rather more than maritime architecture; and he would most certainly have remarked that they were people of a very superior taste as regards their outward appearance.

The young lady was dressed in the height of fashion, for another wind was blowing in 1867: the beginning of a revolt against the crinoline and the large bonnet. The eye in the telescope might have glimpsed a magenta skirt of an almost daring narrowness – and shortness, since two white ankles could be seen beneath the rich green coat and above the black boots that delicately trod the revetment; and perched over the netted chignon, one of the impertinent little flat 'pork-pie' hats with a delicate tuft of egret plumes at the side – a millinery style that the resident ladies of Lyme would not dare to wear for at least another year; while the taller man, impeccably in a light grey, with his top hat held in his free hand, had severely reduced his dundrearies, which the arbiters of the best English male fashion had declared a shade vulgar – that is, risible to the foreigner – a year or two previously. The colours of the young lady's clothes would strike us today as distinctly strident; but the world was then in the first fine throes of the discovery of aniline dyes. And what the feminine, by way of compensation for so much else in her expected behaviour, demanded of a colour was brilliance, not discretion.

But where the telescopist would have been at sea himself was with the other figure on that sombre, curving mole. It stood right at the seawardmost end, apparently leaning against an old cannon-barrel up-ended as a bollard. Its clothes were black. The wind moved them, but the figure stood motionless, staring, staring out to sea, more like a living memorial to the drowned, a figure from myth, than any proper fragment of the petty provincial day.

Chapter 2

> In that year (1851) there were some 8,155,000 females of the age of ten upwards in the British population, as compared with 7,600,000 males. Already it will be clear that if the accepted destiny of the Victorian girl was to become a wife and mother, it was unlikely that there would be enough men to go round.
>
> E. ROYSTON PIKE, *Human Documents of the Victorian Golden Age*

> I'll spread sail of silver and I'll steer towards the sun,
> I'll spread sail of silver and I'll steer towards the sun,
> And my false love will weep, and my false love will weep,
> And my false love will weep for me after I'm gone.
>
> WEST-COUNTRY FOLKSONG: 'As Sylvie was walking'

'My dear Tina, we have paid our homage to Neptune. He will forgive us if we now turn our backs on him.'

'You are not very *galant*.'

'What does that signify, pray?'

'I should have thought you might have wished to prolong an opportunity to hold my arm without impropriety.'

'How delicate we've become.'

'We are not in London now.'

'At the North Pole, if I'm not mistaken.'

'I *wish* to walk to the end.'

And so the man, with a dry look of despair, as if it might be his last, towards land, turned again, and the couple continued down the Cobb.

'And I wish to hear what passed between you and Papa last Thursday.'

'Your aunt has already extracted every detail of that pleasant evening from me.'

The girl stopped, and looked him in the eyes.

'Charles! Now Charles, you may be as dry a stick as you like with everyone else. But you must not be stick-y with me.'

'Then how, dear girl, are we ever to be glued together in holy matrimony?'

'And you will keep your low humour for your club.' She primly made him walk on. 'I have had a letter.'

'Ah. I feared you might. From Mama?'

'I know that something happened ... over the port.'

'They walked on a few paces before he answered; for a moment Charles seemed inclined to be serious, but then changed his mind.

'I confess your worthy father and I had a small philosophical disagreement.'

'That is very wicked of you.'

'I meant it to be very honest of me.'

'And what was the subject of your conversation?'

'Your father ventured the opinion that Mr Darwin should be exhibited in a cage in the zoological gardens. In the monkey-house. I tried to explain some of the scientific arguments behind the Darwinian position. I was unsuccessful. *Et voilà tout.*'

'How could you – when you know Papa's views!'

'I was most respectful.'

'Which means you were most hateful.'

'He did say that he would not let his daughter marry a man who considered his grandfather to be an ape. But I think on reflection he will recall that in my case it was a titled ape.'

She looked at him then as they walked, and moved her head in a curious sliding sideways turn away; a characteristic gesture when she wanted to show concern – in this case, over what had been really the greatest obstacle in her view to their having become betrothed. Her father was a very rich man; but her grandfather had been a draper, and Charles's had been a baronet. He smiled and pressed the gloved hand that was hooked lightly to his left arm.

'Dearest, we have settled that between us. It is perfectly proper that you should be afraid of your father. But I am not marrying him. And you forget that I'm a scientist. I have written a monograph, so I must be. And if you smile like that, I shall devote all my time to the fossils and none to you.'

'I am not disposed to be jealous of the fossils.' She left an artful pause. 'Since you've been walking on them now for at least a minute – and haven't even deigned to remark them.'

He glanced sharply down, and as abruptly kneeled. Portions of the Cobb are paved with fossil-bearing stone.

'By jove, look at this. *Certhidium portlandicum.* This stone must come from the oolite at Portland.'

'In whose quarries I shall condemn you to work in perpetuity – if you don't get to your feet at once.' He obeyed her with a smile. 'Now, am I not kind to bring you here? And look.' She led him to the side of the rampart, where a line of flat stones inserted sideways into the wall served as rough steps down to a lower walk. 'These are the very steps that Jane Austen made Louisa Musgrove fall down in *Persuasion.*'

'How romantic.'

'Gentlemen were romantic ... then.'

'And are scientific now? Shall we make the perilous descent?'

'On the way back.'

Once again they walked on. It was only then that he noticed, or at least realized the sex of, the figure at the end.

'Good heavens, I took that to be a fisherman. But isn't it a woman?'

Ernestina peered – her grey, her very pretty eyes, were shortsighted, and all she could see was a dark shape.

'Is she young?'

'It's too far to tell.'

'But I can guess who it is. It must be poor Tragedy.'

'Tragedy?'

'A nickname. One of her nicknames.'

'And what are the others?'

'The fishermen have a gross name for her.'

'My dear Tina, you can surely –'

'They call her the French Lieutenant's ... Woman.'

'Indeed. And is she so ostracized that she has to spend her days out here?'

'She is ... a little mad. Let us turn. I don't like to go near her.'

They stopped. He stared at the black figure.

'But I'm intrigued. Who is this French lieutenant?'

'A man she is said to have ...'

'Fallen in love with?'

'Worse than that.'

'And he abandoned her? There is a child?'

'No. I think no child. It is all gossip.'

'But what is she doing there?'

'They say she waits for him to return.'

'But ... does no one care for her?'

'She is a servant of some kind to old Mrs Poulteney. She is never to be seen when we visit. But she lives there. Please let us turn back. I did not see her.'

But he smiled.

'If she springs on you I shall defend you and prove my poor gallantry. Come.'

So they went closer to the figure by the cannon-bollard. She had taken off her bonnet and held it in her hand; her hair was pulled tight back inside the collar of the black coat – which was bizarre, more like a man's riding-coat than any woman's coat that had been in fashion those past forty years. She too was a stranger to the crinoline; but it was equally plain that that was out of oblivion, not knowledge of the latest London taste. Charles made some trite and loud remark, to warn her that she was no longer alone, but she did not turn. The couple moved to where they could see her face in profile; and how her stare was aimed like a rifle at the farthest horizon. There came a stronger gust of wind, one that obliged Charles to put his arm round Ernestina's waist to support her, and obliged the woman to cling more firmly to the bollard. Without quite knowing why, perhaps to show Ernestina how to say boo to a goose, he stepped forward as soon as the wind allowed.

'My good woman, we can't see you here without being alarmed for your safety. A stronger squall –'

She turned to look at him – or as it seemed to Charles, through him. It was not so much what was positively in that face which remained with him after that first meeting, but all that was not as he had expected; for theirs was an age when the favoured feminine look was the demure, the obedient, the shy. Charles felt immediately as if he had trespassed; as if the Cobb belonged to that face, and not to the Ancient Borough of Lyme. It was not a pretty face, like Ernestina's. It was certainly not a beautiful face, by any period's standard or taste. But it was an unforgettable face, and a tragic face. Its sorrow welled out of it as purely, naturally and unstoppably as water out of a woodland spring. There was no artifice there, no hypocrisy, no hysteria, no mask; and above all, no sign of madness. The madness was in the empty sea, the empty horizon, the lack of reason for such sorrow; as if the spring was natural in itself, but unnatural in welling from a desert.

Again and again, afterwards, Charles thought of that look as a lance; and to think so is of course not merely to describe an object but the effect it has. He felt himself in that brief instant an unjust enemy; both pierced and deservedly diminished.

The woman said nothing. Her look back lasted two or three seconds at most; then she resumed her stare to the south. Ernestina plucked Charles's sleeve, and he turned away, with a shrug and a smile at her. When they were nearer land he said, 'I wish you hadn't told me the sordid facts. That's the trouble with provincial life. Everyone know everyone and there is no mystery. No romance.'

She teased him then: the scientist, the despiser of novels.

From John Fowles, *The French Lieutenant's Woman*. Copyright © 1969 by John Fowles. London: Jonathan Cape Ltd, 1969. Reprinted by permission of Sheil Land Associates Ltd.

STORY

Development of action (events)

Following Aristotle's *Poetics*, theories of narrative describe a complete story as having a beginning, a middle, and an end. A narrative should be coherent; that is, it should be possible to fit together its events into some kind of meaningful pattern. Analysts sometimes feel a need to distinguish between certain definite phases in the arrangement of narrated events. Often a story begins with an exposition, or an introduction to the action. It may be a description of the setting or of the narrative situation which precedes the beginning of the action. The inciting moment is the first event which suggests the intrigue (action) to follow. The turning point of the action, its most important event, is called a climax. (In some fictional texts there may be several climactic scenes.) In the closure (denouement) of the story, loose ends are tied up, questions answered, and enigmas solved. A text may end with a coda, or a kind of epilogue or conclusion which does not add to the events but constitutes, for instance, a commentary or a reflection on them.[3]

An event can be defined as something that happens. This "something" must be of significance in the development of the plot and can be summed up by a verb or the name of an action. Consider the sentence "She put on her hat and walked out." In one analysis, it may be enough to speak of the event of "leaving";

[3] The set of analytical categories given here is helpful if they are not turned into rigid entities. Moreover, stories do not necessarily develop either through all the phases or in the order described here.

in another, it may be important to identify both events: the act of putting on the hat and the act of leaving.

When the order of events is chronological, such terms as *flash-back* (retrospection) and *foreshadowing* (anticipation) are often used. To avoid the psychological as well as the cinematic–visual connotations of these terms, some critics prefer to name them *analepsis* and *prolepsis*. Analepsis provides past information about a character or event; prolepsis indicates a future event before it actually takes place.[4]

1. In the excerpts provided, identify expositions, inciting moments, instances of flashback and foreshadowing (or, if you prefer, of analepsis and prolepsis) in the stories told in *The French Lieutenant's Woman* and *The Great Gatsby*.

Setting (environment)

For the sake of clarity it is useful to separate the spatio-temporal setting into its environment and time components. The physical surroundings (domestic interiors, streets, landscapes) as well as the social environment (family, social group) often serve to suggest character traits; they also help to establish a mood or suggest the philosophy informing the narrative.

2. Both excerpts offer rather detailed descriptions of the physical setting in which the reader first meets the protagonists. What ideas would you say these descriptions prompt the reader to entertain at the beginning of the narrative?

Time

We can begin by distinguishing the time of the narrated events from the time of narration (story time and narration time). Stories

---

4 These terms have been proposed by the French narratologist Gérard Genette. On the whole, narratologists coin new terms to replace the old ones in order to avoid the commonsensical, psychologizing implications of terms used in traditional poetics. Thus, instead of the term *character*, a narratologist may use the term *actant* to emphasize his/her interest in the laws and logic of narrative rather than in what the narrative is about.

are very often narrated after the events have taken place, so narration time is often chronologically later than the incidents narrated.[5]

3. Identify story time and narration time in the two excerpts. How are the two related? How are they signaled (for instance, by direct reference to dates, or other information which implies time, such as the phrase "the fall of the Berlin Wall")?

Another distinction regarding time is implied by the narratological differentiation between story and plot. Roughly speaking, story implies the strict linear chronological succession of events, and plot an artistically arranged order of events, that is, the order in which the events are narrated.

4. Identify the events mentioned or described in the two excerpts and compare their chronology with the order of their appearance in the texts. While working on the excerpt from *The French Lieutenant's Woman*, focus on Chapter 2, and in the case of *The Great Gatsby*, on the part after the asterisk.

Characters

Fictional characters are verbal constructs and not human beings in the literal sense of the term, yet they are modeled on the writer's and the reader's concept of people and in this sense they are person-like. We speak of direct characterization when a character's quality is named by the narrator, and indirect characterization when a trait is exemplified in the action or the character's own speech or thoughts.

5. How are the characters presented in the two excerpts? What information about their emotions, thoughts, and appearance is

5 According to some narratologists, time may be viewed in three respects: order ("when?"), duration ("how long?"), and frequency ("how often?"). We limit our discussion of time to the aspect of order. Also, while we use the term *plot*, others have used *discourse, narrative,* or *text*.

given? In what way is this information provided? Is it the narrator, other characters, or the character's speech and action that "betray" his/her traits?

NARRATOR

Traditionally, theories of narrative distinguish between first-person and third-person narrators. The narrator may be one of the characters or be placed outside the events of the story. The narrator may be emotionally involved or detached, omniscient (all-knowing) or of limited knowledge. Some narrators are intrusive; that is, they interrupt the narration with direct comments on the narrated events or characters or even on the form of the narration; they may argue a point, instruct the reader, etc. Others may be "impersonal" and "invisible." We can also speak of "reliable" and "unreliable" narrators.

Usually verbalized by the narrator, the story is presented through the mediation of some perspective, angle of vision, or point of view, which in narratology is sometimes called _focalization._ Focalization may be close to, or separate from, the perspective of the narrating agent. Narration and focalization are, for instance, separate in many first-person retrospective narratives in which childhood memories are narrated in the language of an adult but presented (focalized) as experienced by a child.

The setting and time in which the narrator is situated may either vaguely or quite distinctly differ from the spatio-temporal setting of the events.

6. Consider the use of the narrator in the two excerpts: Is the narrator consistently third- or first-person? Does the narrator do both the seeing and the talking, or is the narration conducted from a different angle of vision than the narrator's? Do you see signals of narratorial omniscience, or is the narrator's knowledge of events, characters, setting, etc. limited?

NARRATEE

The narratee is the recipient of the story told by the narrator. Sometimes the narratee is fully personified (a character), or addressed by the narrator as, for instance, "you" or "Madam/Sir." Often, however, the narratee is no more than a silent addressee.

7. Consider the two excerpts for their construction of the narratee. Does the narrator address a definite type of listener directly, or is the listener only indirectly implied? What would you say is the relationship between the narrator and the narratee? For instance, does the narrator confide in the narratee? Does the narrator lecture, instruct, or merely inform him/her? Does the narrator treat him/her as an equal or as a less knowledgeable/intelligent/informed agent?

One of the most popular – perhaps even *the* most popular – form of narrative in the twentieth century is film.[6] As you know, many literary texts have been turned into movies. In fact, over 50 percent of all films made in this century have been based on novels, short stories, or plays. (In a few cases, however, film scripts have been turned into novels, for instance the 1970 best-seller *Love Story* and *The Godfather*.) A number of fiction writers have even worked on film scripts, for instance F. Scott Fitzgerald, William Faulkner, and Harold Pinter.

In its relatively short history, the art of film has undergone many changes due to such technical innovations as the introduction of sound, the use of color, the zoom lens, etc. It is beyond the scope of this unit to present film techniques in any detail, but we would like to mention a few terms which will be useful when working on the tasks below.

The primary unit of expression in film is the image, or the single shot. It is conventional to distinguish between long-distance (panoramic) shots, medium-shots, and close-ups. The

---

6 We use the term *film* to refer to what film theorists call *fiction film*. Strictly speaking, film is of course a broader category which includes the documentary, the animated film, and the experimental film. Fiction film, in turn, includes such genres as the western, the musical, the thriller, the love story, the science-fiction film, etc.

movement on the screen generally seems to be that of "ordinary life," but the shots may be shown in slow or accelerated motion for special effects. For instance, a slow-motion sequence is often used to express dreams, while a fast-motion sequence may be used for comic effect. A single shot may be shown for a long time (freeze-frame) to suggest, for instance, intensity or importance. Usually assumed to be presented in chronological order, the story may be interrupted by flashbacks to relate a significant event to an earlier time, or by flashes forward to interject future events. The scenes can be shot from an upward or downward angle to suggest a point of view. Some critics argue that the camera movement may be treated as "standing for" the narrator in fiction; in any case, it signals the presence of a narrator, a teller of the story. To explain or comment on the action, or render a particular character's feelings or thoughts, written captions or voice-over narration can be used.[7]

When a literary text is turned into a film, it can be said that the "same" story exists as two different narratives. In what follows we will look at two different ways of recoding prose narratives into a visual medium. We will also examine a few differences in the narrative techniques of film and prose fiction.

We begin by looking at the first scenes of the two films, those which precede and run parallel to the printed information (credits) about the films' directors, screenplay writers, titles, etc. These scenes function as equivalents to the expository paragraphs in the two novels.

8. What themes and mood would you say the opening scenes introduce? How do they compare with the themes and mood introduced in the two excerpts you have studied?

Most films do not "tell" their stories in the sense that stories are

---

7   One of the issues much debated in film theory is the question of the positioning of the film spectator. Many feminist theorists claim that the spectator position is coded as "masculine" regardless of the actual sex of any flesh-and-blood moviegoer (see Laura Mulvey's seminal essay "Visual Pleasure and Narrative Cinema"). We discuss the issue of gender-specific reading position in Unit Five.

told in prose narratives, mainly because, as many film theorists point out, films do not have obvious equivalents of fictional narrators. Nevertheless, the directors of the movies based on *The French Lieutenant's Woman* and *The Great Gatsby* chose to signal the narrative voice and perspective in their film adaptations, although they did so in two different ways.

9. As you have noticed, both novels have prominent, voluble, interpreting, and commenting narrators. Check the extent to which the narrators' comments are rendered in the opening scenes of the movie versions. Make a note of how the narrator's perspective is presented in these scenes. (In working on this part of the task, focus on Chapter 1 of Fowles's novel, and in Fitzgerald's on the text preceding the asterisk.) As you have discovered, story time and narration time are not identical in either *The Great Gatsby* or *The French Lieutenant's Woman.* How is the difference between the two signaled in the movies?

The plots of both novels seem to lend themselves with ease to film adaptation. The actors can do roughly what the characters do, and the film dialogues are largely copied from the literary texts. A more challenging task is to render the characters' thoughts and states of mind in a film.

10. Compare the literary and film scenes of Charles's first meeting with Sarah, and Nick's with Daisy and Jordan. The paragraphs we would like you to focus on are marked with a vertical line. How specific are the film scenes in conveying the ideas and feelings described/presented in the literary texts? Which medium would you say offers a more "saturated" presentation of the meeting – that is, which leaves more and which less to the spectator's/reader's imagination?

While prose fiction is a linguistic artifact, in films visual images tend to dominate, supplemented by complex soundtracks of verbal communication, music, and other sounds (for instance, traffic or gunshots). Nowhere is the dominance of visual images clearer than in the case of description. Novels necessarily use verbal descriptions, while films prefer visual representation. A "translation" of a text's descriptive words, phrases, and passages into film images is one of the most basic transformations of the prose narrative into a new medium. The following passage discusses one instance of such transformation:

> Consider the first description of the protagonist in the novel *The French Lieutenant's Woman*: Charles Smithson, as he walks along the quay at Lyme Regis, dressed "impeccably in a light gray, with his top hat in his free hand, had severely reduced his dundrearies." "Dundrearies" are long flowing side-whiskers, named after the character Lord Dundreary in the play *Our American Cousin*. Compared with the rich visual evocation of the film, these details of Charles's appearance are relatively sparse – though precise, because *named*. The film offers a multitude of visual details, more than any viewer could mentally specify; the specification would be in words, and we do not name every detail we see. Further, these details appear simultaneously in the first instant of the sequence. We see not only Charles's sideburns in their full glory but along with them the exact contour and color of his hat, the curl of its brim, the angle of his spread collar and Windsor tie, the precise color and texture of his overcoat and suit coat, his vest and trousers in matching tweed, his darker brown gloves, and so on. Indeed, the film image, as a sign or group of signs of Charles's appearance, *exhausts* the total potential of visible descriptive details. There is no "hole": the image is complete, of a single piece. But for all this plenitude, we still do not know (short of being experts in Victorian fashion) that Charles's sideburns are "dundrearies." (Chatman, p. 39)

11. Compare the texts and their film versions and pick out one or two examples of the kind of transformation that Seymour Chatman describes in the passage quoted above.

The branch of literary theory that studies narrative is called narratology. Narratological interests focus on the structure of texts rather than on their meaning. We could say that narratology emphasizes *how* meaning is created rather than *what* a story means. The basic distinction in narratological studies of the narrative is, as we have mentioned, that between "story" (also referred to as *fabula* or basic story material, that is, the events told and the characters participating in them) and "plot" (also referred to as *sjuzet*, narration, or discourse, that is, the order and manner in which a given story material is rendered). This distinction is theoretically viable, but in practice impossible, since all stories are plotted – all are narrated in a certain way. That is, a "story" cannot occur independently of its "discourse." It may be argued that narratological models are too static, unable to capture the dynamism of story configurations, and reductive in their disregard of such aspects of narrative texts as psychological insights or irony. Whatever the deficiencies of narratology, its influence has been considerable in both literary studies and cultural analysis as well as in philosophy, anthropology, legal studies, etc.

WRITTEN ASSIGNMENT

Choose a short fairy tale (or any other short prose text) that you know well and describe its structure with the help of any of the concepts introduced in this unit that you find useful. You may note, for instance, that the phrase "Once upon a time ..." constitutes an exposition, and consider whether the closing phrase of many tales, "And they lived happily ever after," could be described as an epilogue or coda.

See "Interpretation" in the Glossary.

A plurality of readings: what makes an interpretation acceptable?

In this unit we address the issue of interpretive constraints and accepta-bility. We ask, What induces multiple readings of a given text? Can we speak of "better" and "worse" interpretations? What/who validates an interpretation?

Material:

> *Section One*
> William Wordsworth, "A Slumber Did My Spirit Seal ..." (1800)
> F. W. Bateson, excerpt from *English Poetry* (1950)
> Cleanth Brooks, excerpt from "Irony as a Principle of Struc-ture" (1951)
> J. Hillis Miller, excerpts from *Romanticism and Contemporary Criticism* (1986)

> *Section Two*
> Emily Dickinson, "My Life had stood – a Loaded Gun –" (writ-ten c. 1863)
> Charles R. Anderson, excerpts from *Emily Dickinson's Poetry: Stairway of Surprise* (1960)
> Albert Gelpi, excerpt from "Emily Dickinson and the Deer-slayer" (1979)
> Adrienne Rich, excerpt from "Vesuvius at Home: The Poetry of Emily Dickinson" (1979)
> Shira Wolosky, excerpt from *Emily Dickinson: A Voice of War* (1984)

Section One

William Wordsworth: "A Slumber Did My Spirit Seal ..."

"A slumber did my spirit seal ..."

A slumber did my spirit seal;
I had no human fears:
She seemed a thing that could not feel
The touch of earthly years.

No motion has she now, no force;
She neither hears nor sees;
Rolled round in earth's diurnal course,
With rocks, and stones, and trees.

1800

The purpose of Exercise 1 is to prepare you to evaluate the views of other critics. So it would be best for you not to look at their readings until you have given yourself a chance to determine your own interpretation.

EXERCISE 1

1. After noting features of the poem that interest or puzzle you, what would you say the poem is about?
2. Who do you think "she" refers to? What kind of "slumber" do you think is suggested?
3. Now take a closer look at the text's language. What personal pronouns appear in the text? Underline the verbs and make a note of the tenses used. What are the implications of "seemed"?
4. What contrasts (explicit and implicit) can you find in the poem? What do you think is signaled by the stanza break?
5. What feelings would you say the poem expresses?

EXERCISE 2

1. After you have completed the above tasks, read the following critical statements about Wordsworth's poem. Note your agreements and/or disagreements with the points made.

The final impression the poem leaves is not of two contrasting moods, but of a single mood mounting to a climax in the pantheistic magnificence of the last two lines.... The vague living-Lucy of this poem is opposed to the grander dead-Lucy who has become involved in the sublime processes of nature. We put the poem down satisfied, because its last two lines succeed in effecting a reconciliation between the two philosophies or social attitudes. Lucy is actually more alive now that she is dead, because she is now a part of the life of Nature, and not just a human "thing." (Bateson, pp. 33, 80–81)

[The poet] attempts to suggest something of the lover's agonized shock at the loved one's present lack of motion – of his response to her utter and horrible inertness.... Part of the effect, of course, resides in the fact that a dead lifelessness is suggested more sharply by an object's being whirled about by something else than by an image of the object in repose. But there are other matters which are at work here: the sense of the girl's falling back into the clutter of things, companioned by things chained like a tree to one particular spot, or by things completely inanimate like rocks and stones.... [She] is caught up helplessly into the empty whirl of the earth which measures and makes time. She is touched by and held by earthly time in its most powerful and horrible image. (Brooks, p. 736)

The poem expresses both eloquently restrained grief for [Lucy's] death and the calm of mature knowledge. Before, he was innocent. His spirit was sealed from knowledge as though he were asleep, closed in on himself. His innocence took the form of ignorance of the fact of death. Lucy seemed so much alive, such an invulnerable vital young thing, that she could not possibly be touched by time, reach old age, and die. Her seeming immortality reassured the speaker of his own, and so he did not anticipate with fear his own death. He had no human fears. To be human is to be mortal, and the most specifically human fear, it may be, is the fear of death. (Miller 1986a, p. 103)

2. Now reread the interpretations and identify the words and phrases which signal to you each critic's feelings, emotions, and beliefs. What evidence is there in the poem to support such judgments as "the pantheistic magnificence of the last two lines" (Bateson) or "the lover's agonized shock" (Brooks)? How would you characterize each critic's views on nature, life, and death? How do they compare with your own?

3. Which of the interpretations do you find most convincing? For what reasons?

EXERCISE 3

Read the following critical statement and consider what kind of reader Hillis Miller has in mind, whether you identify yourself with this reader, and what he sees as governing the process of interpretation.

> Any good reader confronted with the words of "A Slumber Did My Spirit Seal ..." will be assailed by a swarm of questions, not by any means faced with a clear, spontaneously generated, construed meaning.... Some of these questions are "grammatical": e.g., why does the poem say "did ... seal" rather than use the simple past tense, "sealed"? Some are "rhetorical" or have to do with tropes: e.g., what does it mean to say someone's "spirit" "slumbers"? what does it mean to say that someone's "spirit" (whatever *that* means in this case) is "sealed"? does it mean as an envelope, or as a bit of wax, or as a tomb, or as someone's lips are "sealed," or what? All of these enigmas are on the same level, so to speak. Each enters into the others, is intertwined with them, so that one cannot be "solved" without the others. (Miller 1986b, p. 15)

You will have noticed that all three critics presuppose that "she" refers to a girl who has died, and that two of them refer to her by the name Lucy. This is because of an editorial decision to print "A Slumber Did My Spirit Seal ..." together with four other poems which all refer to a Lucy. The result of this grouping is that "A Slumber Did My Spirit Seal ..." is also assumed to have reference to Lucy, who has not actually been identified. The decision to include "A Slumber Did My Spirit Seal ..." among the "Lucy poems" is based on the fact that, like all but one of them, it was written in 1799. The poem first appeared in a letter Wordsworth wrote to Coleridge, and Coleridge speculated that it was an epitaph for the imagined death of Wordsworth's sister, Dorothy.

This type of speculation is an example of the way the extrinsic context of a work – here, its placing by an editor in a collection of an author's works – exerts a powerful influence on how it is interpreted. Bateson's reading has also been influenced by a context of another kind, namely his familiarity with the "pantheism" of Wordsworth's other poems. The degree to which this kind of extrinsic information is to be considered valid evidence for an interpretation has been the subject of critical debate since the heyday of New Criticism in the 1940s and 1950s.

Section Two

Emily Dickinson: "My Life had stood – a Loaded Gun –"

754

My Life had stood – a Loaded Gun –
In Corners – till a Day
The Owner passed – identified –
And carried Me away –

And now We roam in Sovreign Woods –
And now We hunt the Doe –
And every time I speak for Him –
The Mountains straight reply –

And do I smile, such cordial light
Upon the Valley glow –
It is as a Vesuvian face
Had let its pleasure through –
And when at Night – Our good Day done –
I guard My Master's Head –
'Tis better than the Eider-Duck's
Deep Pillow – to have shared –

To foe of His – I'm deadly foe –
None stir the second time –
On whom I lay a Yellow Eye –   *Jealousy on the muzzle*
Or an emphatic Thumb –

Though I than He – may longer live
He longer must – than I –
For I have but the power to kill,
Without – the power to die –

c. 1863

EXERCISE 1

1. Read the poem and jot down your preliminary ideas on what you think the poem might be about.
2. Make a note of the images used to present the speaker (the "I") and the "he" of the poem. How would you characterize the relationship between the two?

3. Take another look at the final stanza. What in your opinion is
   the relation between life, death, and killing that the speaker
   describes?
4. Return to the poem and mark the textual moments which you
   find most difficult, unclear, and puzzling.

EXERCISE 2

Now read the critical material on the poem, subjecting each piece
to the kind of close reading that you would perform on a literary
text.

Charles R. Anderson: *Emily Dickinson's Poetry: Stairway of Surprise* (excerpt)

Love is doing as well as being, however, and this opened up new possibili-
ties. Once she found an instrument adequate to render her need for fulfillment through absolute commitment to love's service:

The poem begins with a brilliant conceit. Fused from the ambiguous
abstraction 'Life' and the explicit concretion 'Loaded Gun,' it expresses the
charged potential of the human being who remains dormant until 'identified' into conscious vitality. 'At last, to be identified!' another poem began.
And when she heard of a friend's engagement to be married she wrote:
'The most noble congratulation it ever befell me to offer – is that you are
yourself. Till it has loved – no man or woman can become itself – Of our
first Creation we are unconscious.'

The paradox of finding oneself through losing oneself in love is rendered
in her poem by one word: she achieves *identity* when the lover claims her
as his own. The ecstasy of being swept up into the possession of another led
her once to an extravagant succession of similes. She was borne along
'With swiftness, as of Chariots,' then lifted up into the ether by a balloon,
while 'This World did drop away.' In the gun poem she puts far more in a
single line, 'And carried Me away,' the double meaning encompassing both
the portage of the gun and the transport of the beloved. The first stanza presents a tightly knit unit:

> My Life had stood – a Loaded Gun –
> In Corners – till a Day
> The Owner passed – identified –
> And carried Me away –

Its shock value inheres in the extreme disparity between the two things compared, incongruous in all ways except the startling points of likeness that can be ferreted out. The trap lies in the great precision needed to avoid confusing them, the vital but subjective 'Life' and the objective but inanimate 'Gun.' If she had chosen to use the strict method of metaphysical poetry, the succeeding stanzas would have been devoted to complicating and reconciling these disparities until they coalesce violently in the end.

Instead, after a brief setting introducing her over-image, she proceeds to develop it by the ballad narrative, to which her chosen metrical pattern was so well suited. In another sense, her poem is a domestication on American soil of the tradition of courtly love. The knight has turned pioneer, his quest a hunting expedition in the wilderness, his bower a cabin with feather-pillow and trusty rifle at his head, his lady the frontier wife who shares his hardships and adventures. In such a folk version of the troubadour lyric, the ballad stanza properly replaces the intricate Provençal forms. In the special climate of frontier America, another turn is given to the convention. Since the male provider is unavoidably committed to the strenuous life, here it is the woman who celebrates the softer arts, pledging eternal fidelity and the rapture of love's service. So the courtly roles are reversed: he is only the adored 'Master' while she is the joyous servant, which accounts for her assuming the active role in the love-game.

The hunting action of the second and third stanzas is given over to its devotional aspects. As steadfast companion, her words of love ring out in the gun's explosion, echoed by the mountains; her looks of love are the 'cordial light' of its fire, like the glow of Vesuvius in eruption. The quarry they hunt, 'the Doe,' is appropriate to the romantic theme. But to counterbalance the danger of sentimentalism she makes a pervasive use of hyperbole, suggesting the tall-tale mode of western humor. The protective action of the next two stanzas portrays the service of love. To guard his sleep is better than to share his bed. This may only mean that she places a higher value on giving him peace than on enjoying connubial bliss, though there is a curious suggestion that the love is never fulfilled in physical union. To give him security also calls forth an unquestioning loyalty destructive of his enemies, the jealous anger of the flashing muzzle's 'Yellow Eye' being a particularly happy extension of the image with which she began, the 'Loaded Gun.' Standing for the amorous potential of a newly vitalized life, this has been sustained through all the narrative center, successfully taking the risks inherent in this anatomical-mechanical fusion of part to part – 'speak,' 'smile,' 'face,' and 'eye' applying to the gun as well as to love's servant. With 'thumb' it seems to break down in a shift of agency. Only the 'Owner' has a thumb to raise the hammer, and a finger to fire the gun, but here it fires itself. Her gun-life has so usurped the initiative as to reduce his function to hunting while she herself does the shooting. One of the hazards of the private poet is that the self tends to become the only reality. The lover here certainly plays a negative role.

The final stanza presents a more serious problem to be resolved. A metaphysical poet would have brought his series of shocks to rest in some unexpected figure evolved out of the initial conceit, but her gun only survives in the teasing antithesis of 'kill' and 'die.' A balladist would have rung down the curtain with an ending in surprise comedy or stark tragedy. Instead, she makes a third switch in technique and concludes with an aphorism that seems to have little structural relation to the rest of the poem:

> Though I than He – may longer live
> He longer must – than I –
> For I have but the power to kill,
> Without – the power to die –

If this poem was a deliberate attempt to weld a new form from all these disparate ones – folk ballad, troubadour lyric, tall tale, metaphysical and aphoristic verse – it was a bold experiment even though it did not quite come off. But though the conclusion is a disturbing departure in mode, it may be ventured that its thematic relevance is such as to make it a resolution of all that has gone before. Perhaps this is a poem about the limitations of mortal love and a yearning for the superior glories of the immortal kind. If this is so, then the last stanza is not a moralistic commentary on the narrative but the very meaning which the elaborated image finally creates.

The clues for such an interpretation are not planted thick enough, but there are some. The joys of merely sheltering the beloved are preferred to sharing the marriage bed. And this is the kind of love that finds its expression not in an earthly paradise but in roaming woods that are described here as 'Sovreign,' one of a cluster of words running through her poems to evoke the celestial estate. Earthly love, in spite of the ecstasy of passion and the bliss of service, she was forced to conclude is mortal. Such is the inanimate but loaded gun, once it has been touched into life be being identified by the owner. The physical existence of the gun, her mortal love, may outlast the earthly life of her master, the 'Owner,' but in immortality he will outlive it. So she too must have the 'power to die' into heavenly love in order to become immortal. Limited by her gun-body she has only the 'power to kill,' including paradoxically the soul of the beloved, by making him too enamored of the Eden of this life. In the plaintive 'I have but the power to kill' there may even be the backfire of a suicidal wish, to free him from the encumbrance of her mortal love. It may be reasonably objected that this meaning is too fragmentarily embodied in the poem; and the breakdown of the conclusion into prose brands it, when judged by the highest poetic standards, as a failure. But it is a brilliant one, repaying close study. Moreover, the theme here suggested, though conjectural, is in keeping with the whole trend of her love poetry and will help to illuminate it.

From Charles R. Anderson, *Emily Dickinson's Poetry: Stairway of Surprise.* Copyright © 1960 by Charles R. Anderson.

Albert Gelpi: "Emily Dickinson and the Deerslayer" (excerpts)

In nineteenth-century America there were many women poets – or, I should better say, lady poets – who achieved popular success and quite lucrative publishing careers by filling newspaper columns, gift books, and volumes of verse with the conventional pieties concerning mortality and immortality; most especially they enshrined the domestic role of wife and mother in tending her mortal charges and conveying them to immortality. Mrs. Lydia Sigourney, known as "the Sweet Singer of Hartford," is the type, and Mark Twain's Emmeline Grangerford is the parodic, but barely parodic re-creation. Emily Dickinson was not a lady poet, but she was the only major American woman poet of the nineteenth century – in fact, a poet of such great consequence that any account of women's experience in America must see her as a boldly pioneering and prophetic figure.

In the Dickinson canon the poem which has caused commentators the most consternation over the years is "My Life had stood – a Loaded Gun –." It figures prominently and frequently in *After Great Pain,* John Cody's Freudian biography of Dickinson, and more recently Robert Weisbuch prefaces his explication in *Emily Dickinson's Poetry* with the remark that it is "the single most difficult poem Dickinson wrote," "a riddle to be solved." The poem requires our close attention and, if possible, our unriddling because it is a powerful symbolic enactment of the psychological dilemma facing the intelligent and aware woman, and particularly the woman artist, in patriarchal America....

Despite the narrative manner, it is no more peopled than the rest of Dickinson's poems, which almost never have more than two figures: the speaker and another, often an anonymous male figure suggestive of a lover or of God or of both. So here: I and "My Master," the "Owner" of my life. Biographers have tried to sift the evidence to identify the "man" in the central drama of the poetry. Three draft-"letters" from the late 1850s and early 1860s, confessing in overwrought language her passionate love for the "Master" and her pain at his rejection, might seem to corroborate the factual basis for the relationship examined in this poem, probably written in 1863. However, as I have argued elsewhere, the fact that biographers have been led to different candidates, with the fragmentary evidence pointing in several directions inconclusively, has deepened my conviction that "he" is not a real human being whom Dickinson knew and loved and lost or renounced, but a psychological presence or factor in her inner life. Nor does the identification of "him" as an image symbolic of certain aspects of her own personality, qualities and needs and potentialities which have been identified culturally and psychologically with the masculine, and which she consequently perceived and experienced as masculine.

Carl Jung called this "masculine" aspect of the woman's psyche her "animus," corresponding to the postulation of an "anima" as the "feminine" aspect of the man's psyche. The anima or animus, first felt as the disturbing presence of the "other" in one's self, thus holds the key to fulfillment and can enable the man or woman to suffer through the initial crisis of alienation and conflict to assimilate the "other" into an integrated identity. In the struggle toward wholeness the animus and the anima come to mediate the whole range of experience for the woman and the man: her and his connection with nature and sexuality on the one hand and with spirit on the other. No wonder that the animus and the anima appear in dreams, myths, fantasies, and works of art as figures at once human and divine, as lover and god. Such a presence is Emily Dickinson's Master and Owner in the poem.

However, for women in a society like ours which enforces the subjection of women in certain assigned roles, the process of growth and integration becomes especially fraught with painful risks and traps and ambivalences. Nevertheless, here, as in many poems, Dickinson sees the chance for fulfillment in her relationship to the animus figure, indeed in her identification with him. Till he came, her life had known only inertia, standing neglected in tight places, caught at the right angles of walls: not just *a* corner, the first lines of the poem tell us, but corners, as though wherever she stood was thereby a constricted place. But all the time she knew that she was something other and more. Paradoxically, she attained her prerogatives through submission to the internalized masculine principle. In the words of the poem the release of her power depended on her being "carried away" – rapt, "raped" – by her Owner and Master. Moreover, by further turns of the paradox, a surrender of womanhood transformed her into a phallic weapon, and in return his recognition and adoption "identified" her.

Now we can begin to see why the serious fantasy of this poem makes her animus a hunter and woodsman. With instinctive rightness Dickinson's imagination grasps her situation in terms of the major myth of the American experience. The pioneer on the frontier is the version of the universal hero myth indigenous to our specific historical circumstances, and it remains today, even in our industrial society, the mythic mainstay of American individualism. The pioneer claims his manhood by measuring himself against the unfathomed, unfathomable immensity of his elemental world, whose "otherness" he experiences at times as the inhuman, at times as the feminine, at times as the divine – most often as all three at once. His link with landscape, therefore, is a passage into the unknown in his own psyche, the mystery of his unconscious. For the man the anima is the essential point of connection with woman and with deity.

But all too easily, sometimes all too unwittingly, connection – which should move to union – can gradually fall into competition, then contention and conflict. The man who reaches out to Nature to engage his basic physical and spiritual needs finds himself reaching out with the hands of the predator to possess and subdue, to make Nature serve his own ends. From the point of view of Nature, then, or of woman or of the values of the feminine principle the pioneer myth can assume a devastating and tragic significance, as our history has repeatedly demonstrated. Forsaking the institutional structures of patriarchal culture, the woodsman goes out alone, or almost alone, to test whether his mind and will are capable of outwitting the lures and wiles of Nature, her dark children and wild creatures. If he can vanquish her – Mother Nature, Virgin Land – then he can assume or resume his place in society and as boon exact his share of the spoils of Nature and the service of those, including women and the dark-skinned peoples, beneath him in the established order.

In psychosexual terms, therefore, the pioneer's struggle against the wilderness can be seen, from [that] viewpoint, to enact the subjugation of the feminine principle, whose dark mysteries are essential to the realization of personal and social identity but for that reason threaten masculine prerogatives in a patriarchal ordering of individual and social life. The hero fights to establish his ego-identity and assure the linear transmission of the culture which sustains his ego-identity, and he does so by maintaining himself against the encroachment of the Great Mother. Her rhythm is the round of Nature, and her sovereignty is destructive to the independent individual because the continuity of the round requires that she devour her children and absorb their lives and consciousness back into her teeming womb, season after season, generation after generation. So the pioneer who may first have ventured into the woods to discover the otherness which is the clue to identity may in the end find himself maneuvering against the feminine powers, weapon in hand, with mind and will as his ultimate weapons for self-preservation. No longer seeker or lover, he advances as the aggressor, murderer, rapist.

As we have seen, in this poem Emily Dickinson accedes to the "rape," because she longs for the inversion of sexual roles which, from the male point of view, allows a hunter or a soldier to call his phallic weapon by a girl's name and speak of it, even to it, as a woman. Already by the second stanza "I" and "he" have become "We": "And now We roam in Sovreign woods –/And now We hunt the Doe –," the rhythm and repetition underscoring the momentous change of identity. However, since roaming "in Sovreign Woods –," or, as the variant has it, roaming "the – Sovreign Woods –" is a contest of survival, it issues in bloodshed. "To foe of His – I'm deadly foe," she boasts later, and here their first venture involves hunting the doe. It is important that the female of the deer is specified, for Dickinson's identification of herself with the archetype of the hero in the figure of the woodsman seems to her to necessitate a sacrifice of her womanhood, explicitly the range of personality and experience as sexual and maternal woman. In just a few lines she has converted her "rape" by the man into a hunting-down of Mother Nature's creatures by manly comrades – Natty Bumppo and Chingachgook in *The Last of the Mohicans,* Natty Bumppo and Hurry Harry in *The Deerslayer.*

In the psychological context of this archetypal struggle Emily Dickinson joins in the killing of the doe without a murmur of pity or regret; she wants the independence of will and the power of mind which her allegiance with the woodsman makes possible. Specifically, engagement with the animus unlocks her artistic creativity; through his inspiration and mastery she becomes a poet. The variant for "power" in the last line is "art," and the irresistible force of the rifle's muzzle-flash and of the bullet are rendered metaphorically in terms of the artist's physiognomy: his blazing countenance ("Vesuvian face"), his vision ("Yellow Eye"), his shaping hand ("emphatic Thumb"), his responsive heart ("cordial light"). So it is that when the hunter fires the rifle, "I speak for Him –." Without his initiating pressure on the trigger, there would be no incandescence; but without her as seer and craftsman there would be no art. From their conjunction issues the poem's voice, reverberant enough to make silent nature echo with her words.

In Hebrew the word "prophet" means to "speak for." The prophet translates the wordless meanings of the god into human language. Whitman defined the prophetic function of the poet in precisely these terms: "it means one whose mind bubbles up and pours forth as a fountain from inner, divine spontaneities revealing God.... The great matter is to reveal and out-pour the God-like suggestions pressing for birth in the soul." Just as in the male poetic tradition such divine inspiration is characteristically experienced as mediated through the anima and imaged as the poet's muse, so in this poem the animus figure functions as Dickinson's masculine muse. Where Whitman experiences inspiration as the gushing flux of the Great Mother, Dickinson experiences it as the Olympian fire: the gun-blast and Vesuvius. In several poems Dickinson depicts herself as a smoldering volcano, the god's fire flaring in the bosom of the female landscape. In her first conversation with the critic Thomas Wentworth Higginson, Dickinson remarked: "If I feel physically as if the top of my head were taken off, I know *that* is poetry.... Is there any other way."

But why is the creative faculty also destructive, Eros inseparable from Thanatos? To begin with, for a woman like Dickinson, choosing to be an artist could seem to require denying essential aspects of herself and relinquishing experience as lover, wife, and mother. From other poems we know Dickinson's painfully, sometimes excruciatingly divided attitude toward her womanhood, but here under the spell of the animus muse she does not waver in the sacrifice. Having spilled the doe's blood during the day's hunt, she stations herself for the night ("Our good Day done –") as stiff, soldierly guard at "My Master's Head," scorning to enter the Master's bed and sink softly into "the Eider-Duck's/Deep Pillow." Her rejection of the conventional sexual and domestic role expected of women is further underscored by the fact that the variant for "Deep" is "low" ("the Eider-Duck's/Low Pillow") and by the fact that the eider-duck is known not merely for the quality of her down but for lining her nest by plucking the feathers from her own breast. No such "female masochism" for this doe-slayer; she is "foe" to "foe of His," the rhyme with "doe" effecting the grim inversion.

Moreover, compounding the woman's alternatives, which exact part of herself no matter how she chooses, stands the essential paradox of art: that the artist kills experience into art, for temporal experience can only escape death by dying into the "immortality" of artistic form. The fixity of "life" in art and the fluidity of "life" in nature are incompatible. So no matter what the sex of the deer, it must be remade in the artist's medium; the words of the poem preserve the doe and the buck in an image of their mortality. These ironies have always fascinated and chilled artists. Is the vital passion of the youthful lovers on Keats's "Grecian Urn" death or immortality? In

Eudora Welty's "A Still Moment" Audubon shoots the exquisite white bird so that he can paint it. In John Crowe Ransom's "Painted Head" the artist betrays the young man he has painted by shrinking him into an image. It seems a death's head now, yet this painted head of a now-dead man radiates unaltered health and happiness. No wonder Audubon is willing to shoot the bird. No wonder a poet like Emily Dickinson will surrender to painful self-sacrifice. The loss of a certain range of experience might allow her to preserve what remained; that sacrifice might well be her apotheosis, the only salvation she might know.

Both the poet's relation to her muse and the living death of the artwork lead into the runic riddle of the last quatrain. It is actually a double riddle, each two lines long connected by the conjunction "for" and by the rhyme:

> Though I than He – may longer live
> He longer must – than I –
> For I have but the power to kill,
> Without – the power to die –

In the first rune, why is it that she *may* live longer than he but he *must* live longer than she? The poet lives on past the moment in which she is a vessel or instrument in the hands of the creative animus for two reasons – first, because her temporal life resumes when she is returned to one of life's corners, a waiting but loaded gun again, but also because on another level she surpasses momentary possession by the animus in the poem she has created under his inspiration. At the same time, he *must* transcend her temporal life and even its artifacts because, as the archetypal source of inspiration, the animus is, relative to the individual, transpersonal and so in a sense "immortal."

The second rune extends the paradox of the poet's mortality and survival. The lines begin to unravel and reveal themselves if we read the phrase "Without – the power to die –" not as "lacking the power to die" but rather as "except for the power to die," "unless I had the power to die." The lines would then read: unless she were mortal, if she did not have the power to die, she would have only the power to kill. And when we straighten out the grammatical construction of a condition-contrary-to-fact to conform with fact, we come closer to the meaning: with mortality, if she does have the power to die – as indeed she does – she would not have only the power to kill. What else or what more would she then have? There are two clues. First, the variant of "art" for "power" in the last links "the power to die," mortality, all the more closely with "the power to kill," the artistic process. In addition, the causal conjunction "for" relates the capacity for death in the second rune back to the capacity for life in the first rune. Thus, for her the power to die is resolved in the artist's power to kill, whereby she dies into the hypostasized [*sic*] work of art. The animus muse enables her to fix the dying moment, but it is only her human capabilities, working in time with language, which are able to translate the fixed moment into the words on the page. The artistic act is, therefore, not just destructive but in the end self-creative. In a mysterious way the craftsmanship of the doomed artist rescues her exalted moments from oblivion and extends destiny beyond "dying" and "killing."

Now we can grasp the two runes together. The poet's living and dying permit her to be an artist; impelled by the animus, she is empowered to kill experience and slay herself into art. Having suffered mortality, she "dies into life," as Keats's phrase in *Hyperion* has it; virgin as the Grecian urn and the passionate figures on it, her poetic self outlasts temporal process and those climactic instants of animus possession, even though in the process of experience she knows him as a free spirit independent of her and transcendent of her poems. In different ways, therefore, each survives the other: she mortal in her person but timeless in her poems, he transpersonal as an archetype but dependent on her transitory experience of him to manifest himself. The interdependence through which she "speaks for" him as his human voice makes both for her dependence and limitations and also for her triumph over dependence and limitation.

Nevertheless, "My Life had stood – a Loaded Gun –" leaves no doubt that a woman in a patriarchal society achieves that triumph through a blood sacrifice. The poem presents the alternatives unsparingly: be the hunter or the doe. She can refuse to be a victim by casting her lot with the hunter, but thereby she claims herself as victim. By the rules of the hunter's game, there seems no escape for the woman in the woods.

From Sandra Gilbert and Susan Gubar (eds.), *Shakespeare's Sisters*. Bloomington, Ind.: Indiana University Press, 1979.

Adrienne Rich: "Vesuvius at Home: The Poetry of Emily Dickinson" (excerpt)

There is one poem which is the real "onlie begetter" of my thoughts here about Dickinson; a poem I have mused over, repeated to myself, taken into myself over many years. I think it is a poem about possession by the daemon, about the dangers and risks of such possession if you are a woman, about the knowledge that power in a woman can seem destructive, and that you cannot live without the daemon once it has possessed you. The archetype of the daemon as masculine is beginning to change, but it has been real for women up until now. But this woman poet also perceives herself as a lethal weapon....

[The] poet sees herself as split, not between anything so simple as "masculine" and "feminine" identity but between the hunter, admittedly masculine, but also a human person, an active, willing being, and the gun – an object, condemned to remain inactive until the hunter – the *owner* – takes possession of it. The gun contains an energy capable of rousing echoes in the mountains and lighting up the valleys; it is also deadly, "Vesuvian"; it is also its owner's defender against the "foe." It is the gun, furthermore, who *speaks for him.* If there is a female consciousness in this poem it is buried deeper than the images: it exists in the ambivalence toward power, which is extreme. Active willing and creation in women are forms of aggression, and aggression is both "the power to kill" and punishable by death. The union of gun with hunter embodies the danger of identifying and taking hold of her forces, not least that in so doing she risks defining herself – and being defined – as aggressive, as unwomanly ("and now we hunt the Doe"), and as potentially lethal. That which she experiences in herself as energy and potency can also be experienced as pure destruction. The final stanza, with its precarious balance of phrasing, seems a desperate attempt to resolve the ambivalence; but, I think, it is no resolution, only a further extension of ambivalence.

> Though I than He – may longer live
> He longer must – than I –
> For I have but the power to kill,
> Without – the power to die –

The poet experiences herself as loaded gun, imperious energy; yet without the Owner, the possessor, she is merely lethal. Should that possession abandon her – but the thought is unthinkable: "He longer *must* than I." The pronoun is masculine; the antecedent is what Keats called "The Genius of Poetry."

I do not pretend to have – I don't even wish to have – explained this poem, accounted for its every image; it will reverberate with new tones long after my words about it have ceased to matter. But I think that for us, at this time, it is a central poem in understanding Emily Dickinson, and ourselves, and the condition of the woman artist, particularly in the nineteenth century. It seems likely that the nineteenth-century woman poet, especially, felt the medium of poetry as dangerous, in ways that the woman novelist did not feel the medium of fiction to be.

Reprinted from *On Lies, Secrets, and Silence: Selected Prose 1966–1978* by Adrienne Rich, by permission of the author and W. W. Norton & Company, Inc. Copyright © 1979 by W. W. Norton & Company, Inc.

Shira Wolosky: *Emily Dickinson: A Voice of War* (excerpt)

This poem has prompted many interpretations, which invariably posit Dickinson's psychic life – with regard to poetic, sexual, and/or aggressive energy – as the poem's subject. Its allegory is read accordingly. To Charles Anderson, the Owner is a beloved; the Loaded Gun, "the charged potential of the human being who remains dormant until identified into conscious vitality."[1] To Thomas Johnson, the poet is assessing her poetic achievement, with the poet and her creative power the respective allegorical terms.[2] David Porter similarly sees the gun as "the instrument of language" and the poem as "an allegory, almost pure in self-regard, of language speaking itself."[3] John Cody accepts both the sexual and the poetic readings, but subsumes them into a psychoanalytic reading that emphasizes the link between the "wish to love, to be sexual, to be creative," and "a furious propensity to destroy." The Owner is then "the directing, executive, volitional function," the Gun, "the aggressive, destructive, and erotic impulses."[4] And according to Sharon Cameron, aggressive instinct finally becomes the death instinct and the poem "concerned with the way in which death confers both knowledge and power."[5]

The poem, however, while involving these various psychic forces, may be more literal than has been assumed. Written in 1863, it is perhaps not merely gratuitous that the poem posits firearms as its controlling figure. In this light, the poem's religious resonances may also be taken literally. Preachers were repeatedly insisting that war is a manifestation of divine power, and man, God's instrument in waging it. This could suggest, in a reading posed and rightly dismissed by Cameron, that "picked up by God, the speaker becomes His marksman."[6] For the poem's final recalcitrant stanza – the proof text of any reading – will not sustain the assertion that mortal man has "but the power to kill without the power to die." This seems, instead, a description of the Deity himself – who, like the Gun, has power over life and death and, like the Gun, is himself immortal.

A radical inversion is here implied. The poem's speaker would not be the poet or any human agent, but God; and the poem would examine divine power in conjunction with human agency. Such power is variously suggested. In the second stanza, woods and mountains resound with the Gun's power – a psalmic trope found, for example, in Isaac Watts:

> From mountains near the sky
> Let His high praise resound
> From humble shrubs and cedars high
> And vales and fields around. [54]

That power should also conjoin with wrath is typical of the hymnal and the Bible. For Watts, mountains "shake like frightened sheep" (471). Or as Isaiah prophesies:

> Therefore I will shake the heavens, and the earth shall remove out of her place, in the wrath of the Lord of hosts, and in the day of his fierce anger. And it shall be as the chased doe, and as a sheep that no man taketh up: They shall every man turn to his own people, and flee every one into his own land. [13:13–14]

Dickinson's mountains, like Isaiah's earth, echo with a power that hunts the doe. In the poem, ominous wrath comes in this way to undermine glory. The valley glows at the smile of the All-powerful, but the face remains Vesuvian. The "good Day done" of clerical rhetoric evinces the security felt by those who bestow themselves to heavenly keeping upon lying down to sleep. But here the guardian is lethal.

This power, at least as dreadful as it is majestic, becomes, with the poem's inversion, a human implement. Here, man is not God's instrument, but God man's. In Watts's hymn "For a day of Prayer in time of War," God is called upon to "inspire our armies for the fight" so that "our foes shall fall and die with shame" (602). And the Lord responds: "My sword shall boast its thousands slain / And drink the blood of haughty kings." Here, too, the Gun "to foe of His" is "deadly foe." The Yellow Eye would indeed be deadly if it, as in Watts, "with infinite survey does the world behold" (14) and the thumb, emphatic if found on an Omnipotent hand. But the foe, now, is chosen not by a divine but a human master – a danger perhaps inherent in the topos of a militant church. Murder committed in God's name – as was certainly the case with both northern and southern crusaders – may imply a terrible misuse of heavenly power.

This the poem's conclusion, as parodic rhetoric, suggests:

> Though I than He may longer live
> He longer must – than I
> For I have but the power to kill
> Without the power to die.

Divinity surely lives longer than do mortals. Here, it may be that the divine Gun can deprive of life while remaining immune to death's power. On these grounds, it is further suggested that "He" – here, mortal man – must live longer than the immortal weapon he wields. Perhaps an ascendancy of the human over the divine is intended. Perhaps man, although killing, also experiences death, granting him a certain equity denied to the Gun. Dickinson had earlier written: "Dying – annuls the power to kill." This annulment never overtakes the destructive Creator. That man dies emerges here, as in the earlier poem, as the only positive term – which remains, however, negative. But even that inversion is overshadowed by the poem's central tension and contradiction – that the everliving kills, that the Creator is destructive. The strange counterpoint between innocence and murder for which this poem is famous becomes functional and systematic in the framework of a martial God – who, during the time of this poem's composition, was a concrete and historical, not just a figurative, Being.

The poem's own final attack is directed against that Power which destroys. It may be that man appropriates power to do evil in God's name. But God here seems most blameworthy in the very nature of his power, which is not merely open to misuse, but has wrathful and destructive elements inherent in it. These elements were certainly made painfully evident by the war. And whether the poem is read finally in terms of psychic or divine forces, the problem of destructive power in the order of the world and, therefore, of the contradictions involved in a benevolent and omnipotent God remains preeminent for Dickinson. It extends beyond the fact of war, which finally becomes an instance – and at times a model – for Dickinson's confrontation with evil and suffering. And the theodicy invoked for war, as for suffering in general, becomes less and less satisfactory. War emerges as one aspect of a problem that has for Dickinson broader implications.

1   Charles Anderson, *Emily Dickinson's Poetry: Stairway of Surprise* (New York: Holt, Rinehart & Winston, 1960), p. 174.
2   Thomas Johnson, *Emily Dickinson* (Cambridge, Mass.: Harvard UP, 1955), p. 139.
3   David Porter: *The Modern Idiom* (Cambridge, Mass.: Harvard UP, 1981), pp. 209, 216.
4   John Cody, *After Great Pain* (Cambridge, Mass.: Harvard UP, Belknap Press, 1971), p. 332.
5   Sharon Cameron, *Lyric Time* (Baltimore: Johns Hopkins UP, 1979), p. 71.
6   Cameron, p. 66.

From Shira Wolosky, *Emily Dickinson: A Voice of War*. New Haven, Conn.: Yale University Press, 1984. © 1984 by Yale University. Reprinted by permission.

1. Does the critic present what you would call a coherent reading of the poem? Does he/she signal any interpretive problems? If so, how does the critic go about solving them?
2. What kind of textual and contextual evidence does the critic present to validate the interpretation? What criteria of interpretation do you see each critic follow?
3. Which of the interpretations is/are closest to your own? Which one(s) do you find least convincing? For what reason(s)?
4. Do any of the interpretations of Dickinson's poem seem to be complementary? Do any appear incompatible? In working on this question, you may want to focus on each critic's interpretation of the relationship between the speaker and the "Master" and his/her reading of the final stanza.

Much of the discussion in this unit concerns the language of literary interpretation. According to *Webster's Dictionary*, to *interpret* is derived from the Latin word *interpres*, which means "an agent between two parties, a broker, negotiator." As synonyms for *interpret*, *Webster's* lists the following words: *expound, explain, translate, decipher, construe, unravel, unfold, solve, elucidate*. In literary studies, the agent is a critic who acts as a kind of go-between in matters concerning a literary text and its readers, who, it is assumed, have difficulty understanding the meaning of the text because it is ciphered, folded, and hidden. The interpreter, then, is posited as different from other ("normal"?) readers; he/she is in possession of certain skills and knowledge which allow for an "unraveling" of the meaning.

These skills and knowledge may at times appear to you to be arcane. You may, for instance, have read critical articles whose language you found incomprehensible; you may have been baffled by some interpretations which to you seemed too farfetched, yet which obviously found some degree of approval in the academic community since they were published; you may have been angry when your own interpretation was contested by your teacher or classmates as too idiosyncratic. All or any one of these experiences may have led you to believe that interpretation is a mysterious activity. The exercises in this unit have been designed to help you see interpretation as grounded in historically contingent presuppositions and strategies which are subject to change.

WRITTEN ASSIGNMENTS

1. Make a list of the conventions of interpretation that you see the critics drawing upon in order to validate their readings of the two poems discussed in this unit. (Anderson, for example, refers to the concept of genre, while Gelpi brings forth biographical evidence.)
2. Choose the conventions of interpretation that you find most valid and construct an argument defending them. That means that you must anticipate and answer possible objections to your selection.

See "Interpretation" in the Glossary.

Unit Nine

The question of value

In this unit we consider some of the ways in which our culture attributes value to literary texts. Here "close reading" is not a central activity; instead we look at the texts in the contexts of various cultural "institutions" and "reading communities." We reflect especially on the ideological function of such labels as "high culture" and "low (or mass) culture."

Material:

> Joseph Conrad, excerpt from *Heart of Darkness* (1902)
> William Faulkner, excerpt from *Absalom, Absalom!* (1936)
> Margaret Mitchell, excerpt from *Gone with the Wind* (1936)
> Edgar Rice Burroughs, excerpt from *Tarzan of the Apes* (1912)

According to dictionary definitions, the term *value* may be understood in two basic ways. In one sense, value indicates a monetary equivalent of something. In the other sense, value signals "that quality of a thing according to which it is thought of as being more or less desirable, useful, estimable, important, etc." (*Webster's New Twentieth Century Dictionary*, 1983 ed.). The subject of much philosophical analysis, value is an indispensable concept in everyday life. "No aspect of human life is unrelated to values, valuation, and validations," writes John Fekete (p. i). "Value orientations and value relations saturate our experiences and life practices from the smallest established microstructures of feeling, thought, and behavior to the largest established macro-structures of organizations and institutions" (p. i). In this unit we ask you to consider a few aspects of valuation in the discussion of literature.

1. List approximately 10–15 texts of American and/or English literature (or from any part of the English-speaking world) with which you are familiar. Reflect on your list and answer the following questions:
   a. Which of the texts do you value most and for what reasons?
   b. Which of the texts would you recommend to what kinds of readers?
   c. How did you initially learn about the texts and why did you read them? Were they on your school's reading list? Did you pick them up randomly at a bookstore/library? Did somebody (who?) recommend them?
   d. What is the gender and ethnic background of each author of the texts you have listed?
2. Imagine that you are responsible for designing a one-term course in American and/or English literature for a group of students of your choice (for instance, students in the final year at secondary (high) school or first-term university/college students; native or non-native speakers; etc.). Prepare a list of 10 works that you would like to see taught in the course and be prepared to justify your choices. Then compare your list with the lists prepared by two or three other students. Mark the items which appear on all the lists and then start a process of negotiating the other items in order to come up with a final list of 10 books. What arguments have you used to convince your peers to include the books you suggested? Which of your friends' arguments did you find convincing? Can you specify the values that informed the process of negotiation?
3. Now turn to the texts listed at the beginning of this unit and briefly note what you know about them. Note also where your knowledge about the texts comes from (your own reading? information obtained from a specific source?).

The above questions are meant to make you reflect on some of the ways in which you have acquired knowledge – in this case, of American and English literature. We want to draw your attention to the role of both formal and informal institutions in shaping our sense of what books are worth reading.

In the following set of tasks we ask you to identify what kind of attention the four texts listed above have attracted. This means gathering information of various kinds in a variety of ways.

4. Begin by doing the following:
   a. Check whether the four texts listed at the beginning of the unit are taught in your department/university. In what courses are they listed?
   b. Check how many critical books on them are to be found in your university library. To do this you may consult the library's computer or card catalogue, or go directly to the shelves if your library has an open stacks policy.
   c. Consult the *MLA Bibliography* for three separate years (e.g. 1986, 1990, and 1992) to check how many critical books and articles are listed under the title of each of the texts.

Reflect now on the statistical data you have gathered: Which texts have attracted most attention from the community of academic scholars? Which seem not to have merited the attention of your educational institution and/or scholarly readership? What values does this kind of attention – or its lack – imply?

5. Now do the following:
   a. Check which of the four texts are known to a group of people who do not belong to the "academic community" the way you do. These may be your friends, family, or neighbors, for instance, who have not studied and are not professionally interested in literature. (We suggest that you work in pairs and choose five to ten people.) Try to gather information about what the people you interview value the texts for. Do you share these values?
   b. It is not uncommon for literary texts to be turned into

movies. (You may remember our discussion in Unit Seven.) Find out whether there are film versions of the four texts discussed. How many films have been based on the same text? With which of these films are you familiar?

c. Are there any images (icons) that come readily to your mind in connection with each text? Where would you expect to find these icons? (An example of the kind of image we mean would be, for instance, a lush island that figures in the "desert island" stories, or the face of Marilyn Monroe to signal "sex appeal.")

Reflect on the information you have gathered. Which texts have attracted the most attention from the non-professional reading community? What value does this kind of attention carry in the society at large?

6. Bookstores – especially big ones – arrange the books they sell in different categories, for instance cookbooks, philosophy, gardening, etc. Often these general categories are divided into subcategories; cookbooks can then be classified under, for instance, Italian cooking, dietary cookbooks, vegetarian, cakes and cookies, etc. Check under what categories the four texts discussed may be found in the bookstores you frequent. Are these categories value-laden? If so, in what way(s)?

7. In the close readings of texts in the earlier units, we focused on a number of stylistic and rhetorical strategies. We used such terms as ambiguity, alliteration, repetition, metaphor, literal and figurative language, genre conventions and their mixture, plurality and singularity of meaning, intertextual allusion and parody, and narrative point of view. Using your close reading skills, analyze the opening pages of the four texts reproduced below in terms of any of the above categories you feel are relevant. When you have done this, answer the following questions: Which texts do you find most pleasurable? For what reasons? Which require most analytical labor? For what reasons? What kind of value(s) would you assign to each text?

Joseph Conrad: *Heart of Darkness*

The *Nellie,* a cruising yawl, swung to her anchor without a flutter of the sails, and was at rest. The flood had made, the wind was nearly calm, and being bound down the river, the only thing for it[†] was to come to and wait for the turn of the tide.

The sea-reach of the Thames stretched before us like the beginning of an interminable waterway. In the offing the sea and the sky were welded together without a joint, and in the luminous space the tanned sails of the barges drifting up with the tide seemed to stand still in red clusters of canvas sharply peaked, with gleams of varnished sprits. A haze rested on the low shores that ran out to sea in vanishing flatness. The air was dark above Gravesend, and farther back still seemed condensed into a mournful gloom, brooding motionless over the biggest, and the greatest, town on earth.

The Director of Companies was our captain and out host. We four affectionately watched his back as he stood in the bows looking to seaward. On the whole river there was nothing that looked half so nautical. He resembled a pilot, which to a seaman is trustworthiness personified. It was difficult to realise his work was not out there in the luminous estuary, but behind him, within the brooding gloom.

Between us there was, as I have already said somewhere, the bond of the sea. Besides holding our hearts together through long periods of separation, it had the effect of making us tolerant of each other's yarns – and even convictions. The Lawyer – the best of old fellows – had, because of his many years and many virtues, the only cushion on deck, and was lying on the only rug. The Accountant had brought out already a box of dominoes, and was toying architecturally with the bones. Marlow sat cross-legged right aft, leaning against the mizzen-mast. He had sunken cheeks, a yellow complexion, a straight back, an ascetic aspect, and, with his arms dropped, the palms of hands outwards, resembled an idol. The Director, satisfied the anchor had good hold, made his way aft and sat down amongst us. We exchanged a few words lazily. Afterwards there was silence on board the yacht. For some reason or other we did not begin that game of dominoes. We felt meditative, and fit for nothing but placid staring. The day was ending in a serenity of still and exquisite brilliance. The water shone pacifically; the sky, without a speck, was a benign immensity of unstained light; the very mist on the Essex marshes was like a gauzy and radiant fabric, hung from the wooded rises inland, and draping the low shores in diaphanous folds. Only the gloom to the west, brooding over the upper reaches, became more sombre every minute, as if angered by the approach of the sun.

And at last, in its curved and imperceptible fall, the sun sank low, and from glowing white changed to a dull red without rays and without heat, as if about to go out suddenly, stricken to death by the touch of that gloom brooding over a crowd of men.

Forthwith a change came over the waters, and the serenity became less brilliant but more profound. The old river in its broad reach rested unruffled at the decline of day, after ages of good service done to the race that peopled its banks, spread out in the tranquil dignity of a waterway leading to the uttermost ends of the earth. We looked at the venerable stream not in the vivid flush of a short day that comes and departs for ever, but in the august light of abiding memories. And indeed nothing is easier for a man who has, as the phrase goes, "followed the sea" with reverence and affection, than to evoke the great spirit of the past upon the lower reaches of the Thames. The tidal current runs to and fro in its unceasing service, crowded with memories of men and ships it has borne to the rest of home or to the battles of the sea. It had known and served all the men of whom the nation is proud, from Sir Francis Drake to Sir John Franklin, knights all, titled and untitled – the great knights-errant of the sea. It had borne all the ships whose names are like jewels flashing in the night of time, from the *Golden Hind* returning with her round flanks full of treasure, to be visited by the Queen's Highness and thus pass out of the gigantic tale, to the *Erebus* and *Terror,* bound on other conquests – and that never returned. It had known the ships and the men. They had sailed from Deptford, from Greenwich, from Erith – the adventurers and the settlers; kings' ships and the ships of men on 'Change; captains, admirals, the dark "interlopers" of the Eastern trade, and the commissioned "generals" of East India fleets. Hunters for gold or pursuers of fame, they all had gone out on that stream, bearing the sword, and often the torch, messengers of the might within the land, bearers of a spark from the sacred fire. What greatness had not floated on the ebb of that river into the mystery of an unknown earth!... The dreams of men, the seed of commonwealths, the germs of empires.

The sun set; the dusk fell on the stream, and lights began to appear along the shore. The Chapman lighthouse, a three-legged thing erect on a mud-flat, shone strongly. Lights of ships moved in the fairway – a great stir of lights going up and going down. And farther west on the upper reaches the place of the monstrous town was still marked ominously on the sky, a brooding gloom in sunshine, a lurid glare under the stars.

"And this also," said Marlow suddenly, "has been one of the dark places of the earth."

He was the only man of us who still "followed the sea." The worst that could be said of him was that he did not represent his class. He was a sea-man, but he was a wanderer too, while most seamen lead, if one may so express it, a sedentary life. Their minds are of the stay-at-home order, and their home is always with them – the ship; and so is their country – the sea. One ship is very much like another, and the sea is always the same. In the immutability of their surroundings the foreign shores, the foreign faces, the changing immensity of life, glide past, veiled not by a sense of mystery but by a slightly disdainful ignorance; for there is nothing mysterious to a sea-man unless it be the sea itself, which is the mistress of his existence and as inscrutable as Destiny. For the rest, after his hours of work, a casual stroll or a casual spree on shore suffices to unfold for him the secret of a whole continent, and generally he finds the secret not worth knowing. The yarns of seamen have a direct simplicity, the whole meaning of which lies within the shell of a cracked nut. But Marlow was not typical (if his propensity to spin yarns be excepted), and to him the meaning of an episode was not inside like a kernel but outside, enveloping the tale which brought it out only as a glow brings out a haze, in the likeness of one of these misty halos that sometimes are made visible by the spectral illumination of moonshine.

His remark did not seem at all surprising. It was just like Marlow. It was accepted in silence.

William Faulkner: *Absalom, Absalom!*

From a little after two oclock until almost sundown of the long still hot weary dead September afternoon they sat in what Miss Coldfield still called the office because her father had called it that – a dim hot airless room with the blinds all closed and fastened for forty-three summers because when she was a girl someone had believed that light and moving air carried heat and that dark was always cooler, and which (as the sun shone fuller and fuller on that side of the house) became latticed with yellow slashes full of dust motes which Quentin thought of as being flecks of the dead old dried paint itself blown inward from the scaling blinds as wind might have blown them. There was a wistaria vine blooming for the second time that summer on a wooden trellis before one window, into which sparrows came now and then in random gusts, making a dry vivid dusty sound before going away: and opposite Quentin, Miss Coldfield in the eternal black which she had worn for forty-three years now, whether for sister, father, or nothusband none knew, sitting so bolt upright in the straight hard chair that was so tall for her that her legs hung straight and rigid as if she had iron shinbones and ankles, clear of the floor with that air of impotent and static rage like children's feet, and talking in that grim haggard amazed voice until at last listening would renege and hearing-sense self-confound and the long-dead object of her impotent yet indomitable frustration would appear, as though by outraged recapitulation evoked, quiet inattentive and harmless, out of the biding and dreamy and victorious dust.

Her voice would not cease, it would just vanish. There would be the dim coffin-smelling gloom sweet and oversweet with the twice-bloomed wistaria against the outer wall by the savage quiet September sun impacted distilled and hyperdistilled, into which came now and then the loud cloudy flutter of the sparrows like a flat limber stick whipped by an idle boy, and the rank smell of female old flesh long embattled in virginity while the wan haggard face watched him above the faint triangle of lace at wrists and throat from the too tall chair in which she resembled a crucified child; and the voice not ceasing but vanishing into and then out of the long intervals like a stream, a trickle running from patch to patch of dried sand, and the ghost mused with shadowy docility as if it were the voice which he haunted where a more fortunate one would have had a house. Out of quiet thunderclap he would abrupt (man-horse-demon) upon a scene peaceful and decorous as a schoolprize water color, faint sulphur-reek still in hair clothes and beard, with grouped behind him his band of wild niggers like beasts half tamed to walk upright like men, in attitudes wild and reposed, and manacled among them the French architect with his air grim, haggard, and tatterran. Immobile, bearded and hand palm-lifted the horseman sat; behind him the wild blacks and the captive architect huddled quietly, carrying in bloodless paradox the shovels and picks and axes of peaceful conquest. Then in the long unamaze Quentin seemed to watch them overrun suddenly the hundred square miles of tranquil and astonished earth and drag house and formal gardens violently out of the soundless Nothing and clap them down like cards upon a table beneath the up-palm immobile and pontific, creating the Sutpen's Hundred, the *Be Sutpen's Hundred* like the oldentime *Be Light.* Then hearing would reconcile and he would seem to listen to two separate Quentins now – the Quentin Compson preparing for Harvard in the South, the deep South dead since 1865 and peopled with garrulous outraged baffled ghosts, listening, having to listen, to one of the ghosts which had refused to lie still even longer than most had, telling him about old ghosttimes; and the Quentin Compson who was still too young to deserve yet to be a ghost but nevertheless having to be one for all that, since he was born and bred in the deep South the same as she was – the two separate Quentins now talking to one another in the long silence of notpeople in notlanguage, like this: *It seems that this demon – his name was Sutpen – (Colonel Sutpen) – Colonel Sutpen. Who came out of nowhere and without warning upon the land with a band of strange niggers and built a plantation – (Tore violently a plantation, Miss Rosa Coldfield says) – tore violently. And married her sister Ellen and begot a son and a daughter which – (Without gentleness begot, Miss Rosa Coldfield says) – without gentleness. Which should have been the jewels of his pride and the shield and comfort of his old age, only – (Only they destroyed him or something or he destroyed them or something. And died) – and died. Without regret, Miss Rosa Coldfield says – (Save by her) Yes, save by her. (And by Quentin Compson) Yes. And by Quentin Compson.*

"Because you are going away to attend the college at Harvard they tell me," she said. "So I dont imagine you will ever come back here and settle down as a country lawyer in a little town like Jefferson since Northern people have already seen to it that there is little left in the South for a young man. So maybe you will enter the literary profession as so many southern gentlemen and gentlewomen too are doing now and maybe some day you will remember this and write about it. You will be married then I expect and perhaps your wife will want a new gown or a new chair for the house and you can write this and submit it to the magazines. Perhaps you will even remember kindly then the old woman who made you spend a whole afternoon sitting indoors and listening while she talked about people and events you were fortunate enough to escape yourself when you wanted to be out among young friends of your own age."

Margaret Mitchell: *Gone with the Wind*

Scarlett O'Hara was not beautiful, but men seldom realized it when caught by her charm as the Tarleton twins were. In her face were too sharply blended the delicate features of her mother, a Coast aristocrat of French descent, and the heavy ones of her florid Irish father. But it was an arresting face, pointed of chin, square of jaw. Her eyes were pale green without a touch of hazel, starred with bristly black lashes and slightly tilted at the ends. Above them, her thick black brows slanted upward, cutting a startling oblique line in her magnolia-white skin – that skin so prized by Southern women and so carefully guarded with bonnets, veils and mittens against hot Georgia suns.

Seated with Stuart and Brent Tarleton in the cool shade of the porch of Tara, her father's plantation, that bright April afternoon of 1861, she made a pretty picture. Her new green flowered-muslin dress spread its twelve yards of billowing material over her hoops and exactly matched the flat-heeled green morocco slippers her father had recently brought her from Atlanta. The dress set off to perfection the seventeen-inch waist, the smallest in three counties, and the tightly fitting basque showed breasts well matured for her sixteen years. But for all the modesty of her spreading skirts, the demureness of hair netted smoothly into a chignon and the quietness of small white hands folded in her lap, her true self was poorly concealed. The green eyes in the carefully sweet face were turbulent, willful, lusty with life, distinctly at variance with her decorous demeanor. Her manners had been imposed upon her by her mother's gentle admonitions and the sterner discipline of her mammy; her eyes were her own.

On either side of her, the twins lounged easily in their chairs, squinting at the sunlight through tall mint-garnished glasses as they laughed and talked, their long legs, booted to the knee and thick with saddle muscles, crossed negligently. Nineteen years old, six feet two inches tall, long of bone and hard of muscle, with sunburned faces and deep auburn hair, their eyes merry and arrogant, their bodies clothed in identical blue coats and mustard-colored breeches, they were as much alike as two bolls of cotton.

Outside, the late afternoon sun slanted down in the yard, throwing into gleaming brightness the dogwood trees that were solid masses of white blossoms against the background of new green. The twins' horses were hitched in the driveway, big animals, red as their masters' hair; and around the horses' legs quarreled the pack of lean, nervous possum hounds that accompanied Stuart and Brent wherever they went. A little aloof, as became an aristocrat, lay a black-spotted carriage dog, muzzle on paws, patiently waiting for the boys to go home to supper.

Between the hounds and the horses and the twins there was a kinship deeper than that of their constant companionship. They were all healthy, thoughtless young animals, sleek, graceful, high-spirited, the boys as mettlesome as the horses they rode, mettlesome and dangerous but, withal, sweet-tempered to those who knew how to handle them.

Although born to the ease of plantation life, waited on hand and foot since infancy, the faces of the three on the porch were neither slack nor soft. They had the vigor and alertness of country people who have spent all their lives in the open and troubled their heads very little with dull things in books. Life in the north Georgia county of Clayton was still new and, according to the standards of Augusta, Savannah and Charleston, a little crude. The more sedate and older sections of the South looked down their noses at the up-country Georgians, but here in north Georgia, a lack of the niceties of classical education carried no shame, provided a man was smart in the things that mattered. And raising good cotton, riding well, shooting straight, dancing lightly, squiring the ladies with elegance and carrying one's liquor like a gentleman were the things that mattered.

In these accomplishments the twins excelled, and they were equally out-standing in their notorious inability to learn anything contained between the covers of books. Their family had more money, more horses, more slaves than any one else in the County, but the boys had less grammar than most of their poor Cracker neighbors.

It was for this precise reason that Stuart and Brent were idling on the porch of Tara this April afternoon. They had just been expelled from the University of Georgia, the fourth university that had thrown them out in two years; and their older brothers, Tom and Boyd, had come home with them, because they refused to remain at an institution where the twins were not welcome. Stuart and Brent considered their latest expulsion a fine joke, and Scarlett, who had not willingly opened a book since leaving the Fayetteville Female Academy the year before, though it just as amusing as they did.

"I know you two don't care about being expelled, or Tom either," she said. "But what about Boyd? He's kind of set on getting an education, and you two have pulled him out of the University of Virginia and Alabama and South Carolina and now Georgia. He'll never get finished at this rate."

"Oh, he can read law in Judge Parmalee's office over in Fayetteville," answered Brent carelessly. "Besides, it don't matter much. We'd have had to come home before the term was out anyway."

"Why?"

"The war, goose! The war's going to start any day, and you don't sup-pose any of us would stay in college with a war going on, do you?"

"You know there isn't going to be any war," said Scarlett, bored. "It's all just talk. Why, Ashley Wilkes and his father told Pa just last week that our commissioners in Washington would come to – to – an – amicable agree-ment with Mr. Lincoln about the Confederacy. And anyway, the Yankees are too scared of us to fight. There won't be any war, and I'm tired of hear-ing about it."

"Not going to be any war!" cried the twins indignantly, as though they had been defrauded.

"Why, honey, of course there's going to be a war," said Stuart. "The Yankees may be scared of us, but after the way General Beauregard shelled them out of Fort Sumter day before yesterday, they'll have to fight or stand branded as cowards before the whole world. Why, the Confederacy –"

Scarlett made a mouth of bored impatience.

"If you say 'war' just once more, I'll go in the house and shut the door. I've never gotten so tired of any one word in my life as 'war,' unless it's 'secession.' Pa talks war morning, noon and night, and all the gentlemen who come to see him shout about Fort Sumter and States' Rights and Abe Lincoln till I get so bored I could scream! And that's all the boys talk about, too, that and their old Troop. There hasn't been any fun at any party this spring because the boys can't talk about anything else. I'm mighty glad Georgia waited till after Christmas before it seceded or it would have ruined the Christmas parties, too. If you say 'war' again, I'll go in the house."

She meant what she said, for she could never long endure any conversation of which she was not the chief subject. But she smiled when she spoke, consciously deepening her dimple and fluttering her bristly black lashes as swiftly as butterflies' wings. The boys were enchanted, as she had intended them to be, and they hastened to apologize for boring her. They thought none the less of her for her lack of interest. Indeed, they thought more. War was men's business, not ladies', and they took her attitude as evidence of her femininity.

From Margaret Mitchell, *Gone with the Wind.* New York: Warner Books, 1993. Copyright 1936 by the Macmillan Company; renewed 1964 by Stephen Mitchell and Trust Company of Georgia as Executors of Margaret Mitchell Marsh.

Edgar Rice Burroughs: *Tarzan of the Apes*

Out to Sea

I had this story from one who had no business to tell it to me, or to any other. I may credit the seductive influence of an old vintage upon the narrator for the beginning of it, and my own skeptical incredulity during the days that followed for the balance of the strange tale.

When my convivial host discovered that he had told me so much, and that I was prone to doubtfulness, his foolish pride assumed the task the old vintage had commenced, and so he unearthed written evidence in the form of musty manuscript, and dry official records of the British Colonial Office to support many of the salient features of his remarkable narrative.

I do not say the story is true, for I did not witness the happenings which it portrays, but the fact that in the telling of it to you I have taken fictitious names for the principal characters quite sufficiently evidences the sincerity of my own belief that it *may* be true.

The yellow, mildewed pages of the diary of a man long dead, and the records of the Colonial Office dovetail perfectly with the narrative of my convivial host, and so I give you the story as I painstakingly pieced it out from these several various agencies.

If you do not find it credible you will at least be as one with me in acknowledging that it is unique, remarkable, and interesting.

From the records of the Colonial Office and from the dead man's diary we learn that a certain young English nobleman, whom we shall call John Clayton, Lord Greystoke, was commissioned to make a peculiarly delicate investigation of conditions in a British West Coast African Colony from whose simple native inhabitants another European power was known to be recruiting soldiers for its native army, which is used solely for the forcible collection of rubber and ivory from the savage tribes along the Congo and the Aruwimi.

The natives of the British Colony complained that many of their young men were enticed away through the medium of fair and glowing promises, but that few if any ever returned to their families.

The Englishmen in Africa went even further: saying that these poor blacks were held in virtual slavery, since when their terms of enlistment expired their ignorance was imposed upon by their white officers, and they were told that they had yet several years to serve.

And so the Colonial Office appointed John Clayton to a new post in British West Africa, but his confidential instructions centered on a thorough investigation of the unfair treatment of black British subjects by the officers of a friendly European power. Why he was sent, is, however, of little moment to this story, for he never made an investigation, nor, in fact, did he ever reach his destination.

Clayton was the type of Englishman that one likes best to associate with the noblest monuments of historic achievement upon a thousand victorious battlefields – a strong, virile man – mentally, morally, and physically.

In stature he was above the average height; his eyes were gray, his features regular and strong; his carriage that of perfect, robust health influenced by his years of army training.

Political ambition had caused him to seek transference from the army to the Colonial Office and so we find him, still young, intrusted with a delicate and important commission in the service of the Queen.

When he received this appointment he was both elated and appalled. The preferment seemed to him in the nature of a well-merited reward for painstaking and intelligent service, and as a stepping stone to posts of greater importance and responsibility; but, on the other hand, he had been married to the Hon. Alice Rutherford for scarce a three months, and it was the thought of taking this fair young girl into the dangers and isolation of tropical Africa that dismayed and appalled him.

For her sake he would have refused the appointment; but she would not have it so. Instead she insisted that he accept, and, indeed, take her with him.

There were mothers and brothers and sisters, and aunts and cousins to express various opinions on the subject, but as to what they severally advised history is silent.

We know only that on a bright May morning in 1888, John, Lord Greystoke, and Lady Alice sailed from Dover on their way to Africa.

A month later they arrived at Freetown where they chartered a small sailing vessel, the *Fuwalda,* which was to bear them to their final destination.

And here John, Lord Greystoke, and Lady Alice, his wife, vanished from the eyes and from the knowledge of men.

Two months after they weighed anchor and cleared from the port of Freetown a half dozen British war vessels were scouring the south Atlantic for trace of them or their little vessel, and it was almost immediately that the wreckage was found upon the shores of St. Helena which convinced the world that the *Fuwalda* had gone down with all on board, and hence the search was stopped ere it had scarce begun; though hope lingered in longing hearts for many years.

The *Fuwalda,* a barkantine of about one hundred tons, was a vessel of the type often seen in coastwise trade in the far southern Atlantic, their crews composed of the offscourings of the sea – unhanged murderers and cutthroats of every race and every nation.

The *Fuwalda* was no exception to the rule. Her officers were swarthy bullies, hating and hated by their crew. The captain, while a competent seaman, was a brute in his treatment of his men. He knew, or at least he used, but two arguments in his dealings with them – a belaying pin and a revolver – nor is it likely that the motley aggregation he signed would have understood aught else.

From Edgar Rice Burroughs, *Tarzan of the Apes.* Copyright Edgar Rice Burroughs Inc., Tarzana, Calif.

8. Compare your answers to questions 4, 5, and 6 with your response to question 7. Do you see any correlation between the

formal organization of the text and its theme(s), and its appreciation by the professional and the non-professional reading community?

Traditionally, in literary theory value was understood as something that marks off "great" or "genuine" works of literature from popular or even "non-literary" texts. Thus, the very concept of "literature" or "literary text" bears value judgments: literature is a kind of writing which has more (aesthetic) value than other kinds, for instance letters or newspaper articles. Value is often perceived as something residing in the text, as its inherent property. One of the dominant tacit assumptions concerning inherent literary value has been its association with complex, "difficult," highly structured texts which offer insights into important philosophical and existential questions of significance to (all) people for all time.

Today many critics argue that literary value is not an inherent quality of texts but a function of reading, that is, that we construct the text's value by subjecting it to complex readings and then this complexity of reading is made to stand for the text's complexity. Others conceive of literary value as a conjunction of the complexity of the text with that of its interpretation. This is what Antony Easthope writes: "literary value is a function of the text/reading relation; and history has ... demonstrated that some texts are better than others not because they are always read the same but because they are always read differently" (p. 336).

The idea of close reading – and indeed interpretation itself – is grounded in the belief that some texts are not immediately accessible: their meaning and structure need to be explicated by a specialist. That is, close reading is most often associated with "difficult," "complex," or "deep" texts. Such texts are often codified as "masterpieces" and enter the literary canon.

Some critics argue that it is criticism that creates the category of texts called masterpieces. According to this view, a text begins to be called a masterpiece (or a great/important text) when a great number of critical readings have been produced on its themes, structure, meaning, place in literary history, relation to other cultural texts, etc. Yet this multiplicity of readings, other critics observe, is always linked to the complexity of the text under examination. Still others argue that it is the new reading paradigms that allow readers to perceive complexity where relative simplicity was seen before. The psychoanalytic paradigm, for instance, has generated complex readings of Edgar Allan Poe's "simple" Gothic short stories; the feminist approach to literature has allowed for a complex rereading of a number of texts classified as popular literature, for example Colleen McCullough's best-seller *The Thorn Birds*.[1] This is how one critic answers the question what constitutes a masterpiece:

> the more artistically complex and original a work of art ... the greater is its availability to different readings on both the synchronic and diachronic levels. Or rather, that quality of presence, that sense of perennial contemporaneity and universality produced by a masterpiece, results from the fact that the polysemic weight of the text allows it to be "used" in functions of the literary – and, above all, the socio-ideological – models of various eras. Every era applies its own reading codes, its changed vantage points; the text continues to accumulate sign possibilities which are communicative precisely because the text is inside a system in movement. (Corti, pp. 5–6)

Our own questions in this textbook also signal values: We have asked you to perform close reading on various texts because we find the skill of close reading helpful in constructing a convincing interpretation. We have asked you to reflect on your reading's ideological and critical assumptions because we believe that self-awareness empowers you to question other interpretations. The questions we have formulated, the words we have used, signal our preferences, our ideals, our judgments – and hence our values.

---

1 Of all the psychoanalytic-inflected articles on Poe's short stories, perhaps the best known is Jacques Lacan's "Seminar on 'The Purloined Letter,'" which initiated a series of responses (from, among others, Jacques Derrida and Barbara Johnson) collected in *The Purloined Poe*, ed. John P. Muller and William J. Richardson. McCullough's *The Thorn Birds* has been analyzed by Cora Kaplan in "*The Thorn Birds*: Fiction, Fantasy, Femininity." An important work on popular literature for women is Janice Radway's *Reading the Romance*.

In recent years the question of value has been recast in terms of acts of evaluation. That is, value is not understood as something inherent in texts, but as produced by various (implicit and explicit) acts and practices of evaluation. Among the practices of valuation are reviews in professional and popular magazines and newspapers; curricula choices; and choices of what is published, quoted, reprinted, staged, and awarded literary prizes. In our culture certain people are endowed with more authority than others to pass value judgments. For instance, if a literary critic writes in a known journal (say, *The New York Review of Books* or *Times Literary Supplement*) that "Toni Morrison is a good writer," his/her statement carries more weight than the same statement made by a university undergraduate. Even such seemingly "obvious" statements as, for instance, "*Macbeth* is a great play" can and should be examined critically in terms of the implied values: Great for whom? Great compared with what other plays/works of art? Great in what sense? In other words, today we tend to approach value as constructed rather than inherent: a masterpiece is a literary text which is highly valued by *certain* people in a *specific* cultural context. As a construct, value is subject to change. *Macbeth*, for instance, may not be considered a masterpiece at some point in time.

The distinctions made between various types of texts are not neutral either. For instance, a comic strip or a thriller is considered of less value than a tragedy or a "classic" novel; books for children are valued less than books for educated adults; and poetry is more valued than lyrics written for pop music groups. In the last decades many literary critics have also noted that the vast majority of texts most valued in our culture have been written by male, white, middle-class, Protestant writers. This raises the question of the role of gender, ethnicity, class, and religion in the construction of value.

The kind of distinctions we have mentioned in the preceding paragraph follows value criteria traditionally endorsed by the community of literary scholars. Other reading communities may value literature for children rather than drama, comic strips rather than poetry, film rather than fiction, or detective stories rather than, say, modernist novels. The distinction often made is that between high and popular (or mass) culture. In our culture reading for consumption or immediately obtainable pleasure continues to be perceived as less valuable than reading for knowledge or delayed gratification. That is, pleasure and satisfaction achieved as a result of labor (for instance, after an intense analytical activity) is supposed to be of superior value to the effortless enjoyment of a text.

WRITTEN ASSIGNMENTS

1. Find two (or more) examples of graffiti and write a short essay entitled "Is graffiti a modern art form?" After you have written the essay, check it for the kinds of arguments you have used to answer the question and list them at the end of your essay. By the "kinds of arguments" we mean, for example, appeals to aesthetic value, praise of realistic (or imaginative) presentation of an experience, emphasis on a pleasurable or exciting experience, the pointing out of educational/informative aspects of the text, the consideration of avant-garde forms of expression, etc.

2. Select a song you enjoy listening to and analyze its lyrics (text). Using this analysis write a short essay in which you try to convince the reader of the song's value.

3. Read the two critical responses to the Tarzan stories reprinted below.

the appeal of the Tarzan stories was and is certainly not a literary one, for Burroughs just about totally ignored all the basic rules of style, grammar and syntax. To say that his writing was technically inept would be an understatement. (Ewen, p. 57)

I see Burroughs as a fine artist in his genre of heroic fantasy. His peculiar literary skill is, like Homer's, his ability to combine fantastic and unbelievably exciting adventure stories with commentary on man and his condition. His use of language and literary technique was deeply influenced by his familiarity with the classical languages and literatures. (Holtsmark, p. 6)

As you see, both critics focus on Burroughs's language and technique to justify their assessment of the Tarzan stories, but arrive at radically different conclusions. Drawing upon the results of Exercise 7, write one positive and one negative evaluation of one of the texts excerpted in this unit. Then ask yourself what concepts of literary style and technique have informed each evaluation? Which of the evaluations expresses your convictions? Did you feel any resistance to taking one of your two positions?

See "Discourse" and "Canon" in the Glossary.

Glossary

Note: None of the concepts introduced in the Glossary are simple; none can be defined in an unproblematic way. Various critical schools and theorists define and use the concepts in slightly different ways; these differences, however, are not significant for the purposes of this book.

Binary oppositions

The concept of binary oppositions as it was first developed in structuralist linguistics is central to structuralist poetics and poststructuralist theories. Simply put, a binary opposition is a contrast formed between two elements which function as each other's opposites. For instance, on the phonetic level Ferdinand de Saussure describes the voiced *b* and the unvoiced *p* as binary opposites which distinguish such words as *bet* and *pet*. Similarly, in the system of relations which Claude Lévi-Strauss saw as constitutive of cultures and their myths, such oppositions as *raw* vs. *cooked* and *vengeance* vs. *forgiveness* are examples of the principles which in his view structure a particular reality as it is perceived by a given culture.

While structuralist approaches to language, literature, and culture see the two terms that enter each binary opposition as equal, poststructuralist theory points to the way one of the terms in each pair tends to be culturally marked as positive and the other as negative. In Western culture, for instance, *white* usually carries positive connotations (e.g. of purity and innocence), while *black* carries negative ones (of dirt, evil, and danger). Several theorists have focused on the ideology of the *white/black* and *Occident/Orient* oppositions in order to show how the privileging of the terms *white* and *Occident* permeates Western thinking.

The ideology of binary oppositions has been the subject to much feminist critique. In *The Second Sex* Simone de Beauvoir described patriarchal society as defining *woman* as *not man,* that is, as an inferior "Other." The French feminist Hélène Cixous has pointed out how many binary oppositions in Western culture underlie the opposition *man/woman,* for instance *active/passive, sun/moon, culture/nature,* and *head/heart.* She maintains that these oppositions form a hierarchy in which the feminine is seen as the negative pole of a masculine norm.

Canon

The word *canon* was first used to refer to an authoritative list of the books of the Bible. The selection made by the early church fathers reflected their desire to distinguish the orthodox from the heretical, hence their concern with the conformity of the text's "message" to the beliefs and values of the religious community. The aesthetic value of the texts was not an important aspect of biblical canon formation.

In the process of "canonization" of literary texts, however, it was their aesthetic value and assumed universality of their appeal that were evoked. "Great books" or "classics" formed a body of literature that allegedly represented the best ever written. The attempt to distinguish the enduring from the ephemeral resulted in the construction of a canon which was regarded as – and in some quarters still is – the core of a liberal education.

In recent years the process of canon formation has come under intense scrutiny. Some of the questions to which a variety of answers have been offered are these: How does a work become canonical? What are the mechanisms of exclusion in canon formation? Are acts of aesthetic judgment correlated with the categories of gender, race, and class? What social groups have the authority to decide what good literature is? Whose social interests and identities do canonical works represent?

Many feminist critics as well as critics involved in minority/ethnic studies have noticed that in the category of "great" Western European authors, there have been few women and even fewer writers who are non-white or of lower-class origin. Some critics have advocated "opening the canon" to include women and minority writers, while others have actively worked on forming alternative canons.

Most debates about the canon recognize the importance of *academia* and its curriculum in disseminating knowledge of literature. Areas of current investigation are the institutional practices involved in determining the criteria of cultural literacy, the motives for preserving some works rather than others, and the systems of rewarding some readings and penalizing others. To further investigate the process of canon formation, critics are also studying the history of production and distribution of literary works as well as the various ways they have been read and taught.

Code

The concept of the code is used in a wide variety of contexts. We hear of genetic codes, kinship codes, legal codes, linguistic codes, literary codes, etc. The word *code* is sometimes used as a synonym for *rule* or *system;* sometimes it seems to mean *an organization.* In the context of this book we offer the following definition: A code is a culturally established relationship between a sign and a meaning. For example, the sign for "ladies" when on a door is deciphered as meaning "a restroom (toilet) for women" thanks to a social and cultural agreement (code) that permits such a connection. Codes may be very simple (for instance, correlating the visual sign of a red light with the meaning "danger" in the system of traffic regulations) or very elaborate (for instance, the theatrical code which may be said to consist of a number of subcodes of lighting, staging, music, costumes, gestures, make-up, etc.). The main point is that the rules that establish the correlation between a physical or material sign and its meaning are historically and socially determined. They are, therefore, changeable. That is what is meant when we say that codes are culture-specific.

The most influential scholar in the area of codes and coding in human life and in culture has been Roland Barthes. Barthes has studied the codification of food, clothing, furniture, and other aspects of life in modern France. (See, for instance, *Mythologies*, 1972, or *The Fashion System*, 1983.) Let us take the food system. Barthes gives the example of a restaurant menu. The menu is organized paradigmatically (horizontally) and syntagmatically (vertically). When we compose a meal, we follow the rule of a *syntagmatic* arrangement; that is, we decide that the various food items are to be eaten in a certain order. A starter (appetizer) is supposed to come first, the main dish after the starter but before a dessert, etc. But before we arrange the order in which the food is to be eaten, we have to select an appetizer, main dish, dessert, and beverage from a group of possible starters, main courses, desserts, and beverages. That is, when we look at each group separately in order to make our selection, we explore the *paradigmatic* organization of the food items on the menu. It is possible to break the rules, of course, and order two appetizers but skip the main course. Such an arrangement of one's meal is, however, felt as unorthodox, or "ungrammatical." The "grammars of food coding" differ from culture to culture. In the United States, it is "grammatical" to order a salad before the main course; in France the salad's "proper" place is after the main dish.

To give another example, clothing codes, besides correlating body parts and pieces of clothing, relate clothing and gender, age, social occasion (take the difference in dress between a wedding and a work-out session), social status, etc. Such codes may be more or less explicit and more or less flexible.

In literary criticism one of the famous examples of an extensive use of the concept of code in textual interpretation is Barthes' reading of Balzac's story "Sarrasine" in *S/Z* (1974). As Barthes explains, a code represents a sort of bridge between the text discussed and all other texts. Each text is a point of convergence for numerous codes. Discussing "Sarrasine," Barthes works with five codes: The proairetic code establishes sequences of action. The hermeneutic code articulates and resolves enigmas. The connotative code defines persons and places. The symbolic code establishes unresolvable oppositions. The cultural codes are numerous and heterogeneous; the textual context helps to determine which cultural codes are operative at any given point.

The concept of code has been extensively discussed by scholars interested in semiotics, such as Umberto Eco, the Italian semiotician and philosopher of language, in, for instance, *Semiotics and the Philosophy of Language* (1984). The poststructuralist inquiry into reading and interpretation has both reaffirmed the usefulness of the concept and revealed its limits. This is how one critic presents Jacques Derrida's and Paul de Man's insights concerning the function of codes in reading:

> Both Derrida and de Man assume that the reading of a text will largely be controlled by grammatical and logical codes and by codelike protocols of interpretation established over the centuries and most visibly institutionalized today in the modern university. Yet the insight both regularly educe is that the more deliberately and assiduously one reads a text according to such controls, the less determinable its meanings and effects seem to be. (Stonum, p. 399)

Discourse

The concept of discourse is used to designate a number of things and is common to both linguistics and critical theory. Any language unit – either spoken or written – with an identifiable communicative function may be called a discourse (or a text). The term is also used to refer to types of language use; we speak, for instance, about "literary discourse," "philosophical discourse," and "medical discourse." In poetics, it has been used in such expressions as the "novelistic discourse" to identify the common features of a certain kind of language use.

In much of critical theory today, the term discourse is used in a different sense, that suggested by the work of the French philosopher Michel Foucault. As used by him and his followers, language use is conceived in relation to social institutions and is seen as an instrument of power. Discourses produce knowledge about human beings and their society. Discourses change their form and significance depending on who is speaking, what the speaker's position of power is, and in which institutional context the speaker is situated.

The concept of discourse has also had an impact on how we view literature and the critical activity itself. In certain types of literary criticism the concept has been associated with questions about the ways language works to produce knowledge rather than with the meaning of literary texts themselves. Literary scholars of this persuasion thus resituate literary texts among the social and ideological discourses of their time of production and/or reception. Within the framework of this view, the individual literary work is perceived as an "intertextual weaving" of many discourses other than that of the author.

Ethnic studies

Multicultural literary studies emerged from social and political movements within the academy in the 1960s, especially in the United States. Women and ethnic groups began to demand certain changes in the field of literary studies. They argued, for instance, for the introduction of literatures written by women and "minority" writers into university curricula. This moved critical attention away from formal issues (e.g. "literariness") to issues of the representation of race and gender, that is, to the contextualization of literature. Gradually, scholars began to theorize about the nature and function of literatures which could be called ethnic.

These theories hinge on the understanding of the term *ethnic*. Among the questions much debated today are these: What makes "ethnic literature" (African-American, Native American, or Chicano, for instance) distinct from the literature of the "dominant" culture? Does it have certain innate characteristics, a definite poetics of its own, or is ethnic literature simply literature written by an author belonging to an ethnic group? Are authors always spokespersons for their ethnic groups? What if authors do not identify themselves with their ethnic groups? Can we distinguish between different "ethnic literary codes"? What does it mean to read from an ethnic-specific position? The answers given to these questions vary, but although the field of ethnic studies is a site of struggle, it is definitely on the rise as the issues it concerns itself with are debated more and more in countries other than the United States and Great Britain.

Feminist and gender studies

Although gender studies is sometimes used as an alternative name for feminist studies, the two cannot be simply collapsed onto each other. Feminist and gender studies share a central concern with gender, but while feminist studies focus on women, gender studies is an umbrella term that groups together women's studies, men's studies, and gay and lesbian studies.

Crucial to feminist studies is the distinction between sex and gender. *Sex* is used to refer to a certain group of irreducible, biological differentiations between members of the human race. Sex, then, is grounded in biology. *Gender* is used to denote the culturally prescribed roles and behavior patterns available to the two sexes. While the male/female distinction is perceived as universal, what is typically "masculine" or "feminine" within a given culture is subject to change. As Simone de Beauvoir put it, "One is not born, but rather becomes, a woman" (p. 295). In other words, we learn what is expected of us in order to be women or men: how to dress, what professions to choose, what roles to play, etc.

This understanding of gender as a social construct pinned to a sexed body is fundamental to feminist studies, which, however, does not form a unified field. In literary criticism, the sex/gender problematics have resulted in several distinct areas of interest.

Noticing the relative absence of women among authors whose works have entered the canon of Western literature, some feminist critics have set as one of their tasks the reinscription of women writers into literary history. The study of women writers to reclaim the forgotten legacy of women authors is often referred to as *gynocriticism* (Elaine Showalter's term). Virginia Woolf's *A Room of One's Own* (1929) is often viewed as having initiated interest in the history of women's writing.

Other feminist critics, having found much canonical literature overtly misogynist and oppressive to women, have focused on the issue of the representation of women in literature. The study of the representation of women, called *feminist critique* (or *images of women in criticism*), is often seen as having been originated by Simone de Beauvoir's *The Second Sex* (published in French 1949; first English translation 1953). Having studied several modern male authors, Beauvoir came to the conclusion that female characters tend to be reduced to two types, the angel-mother and the monster-whore. The American feminist critics Sandra Gilbert and Susan Gubar found a recurrent figure of the madwoman or monster in the works of canonical women writers, and saw it as a means of expressing the female writer's anxiety and rage and the "schizophrenia of authorship" (p. 78). Inspired by feminism, some critics have studied constructions of masculinity and have scrutinized the homophobia inscribed in literature and culture. (Eve Kosofsky Sedgwick's *Between Men,* published 1985, is a seminal work in this area.)

Yet another group of feminist critics (most notably Julia Kristeva, Hélène Cixous, and Luce Irigaray), influenced by poststructuralist theories of language, focus on the operation of sexual difference in writing. They investigate linguistic differences in women's and men's writing, and often ground these textual differences in the author's sexuality. This belief in the bodily grounding of linguistic difference is referred to as *écriture féminine*.

In the mid-eighties feminist studies was supplemented by what has come to be called gender studies. It was Michel Foucault's work (especially his *History of Sexuality,* published in French 1976 and in English 1978) that led to a rethinking of the distinction between gender and sexuality. According to Foucault, sexuality as a concept was *invented* in nineteenth-century Europe. Gender rather than sex, then, must be treated as a universal category, although of culturally inflected variations. If this is the case, then the usefulness of the distinction between gender and sex that has been fundamental to feminist theory becomes questionable. Many critics were quick to observe that the binary sexual model of male/female, paired by the gender binarism of masculine/feminine, privileges heterosexuality and marginalizes other forms of desire (gay or lesbian). Arguing that sexual difference is culturally constructed and that there is nothing outside or before culture, some theorists point out that sex is always already gender.

Genre

The word *genre* comes from Greek *genus* and means "kind" or "sort." It implies the possibility of categorizing into groups which share (some) characteristics. The selection of characteristics for purposes of classification is a complex process, most often messy rather than "neat."

In literary studies the classical propositions concerning genre theory were offered by Aristotle and Horace. They suggested that literary texts can be sorted into three fundamental kinds: lyric, epic, and drama. Today we speak of poetry, fiction, and drama. These three kinds of texts are subclassified into various genres. Examples within fiction are the historical, psychological, science-fiction and detective novel (but also the short story, novella, short story cycle, etc.); within the lyric, the ballad, sonnet, elegy, ode, and personal lyric; within drama, tragedy, comedy, farce, and "theater of the absurd." It is easy to see that the codification of texts does not follow a consistent criterion or set of criteria. For instance, in classifying sonnets and villanelles, the poems' formal properties (number of lines and stanzaic patterns) are crucial, while subject matter and tone are operative criteria in classifying some poems as elegies. The ways of defining different genres, their historical evolution, and even the usefulness of preserving the concept have been discussed by many critics.

Genre expectations are often tacit, yet they are among the most powerful horizons of expectations that regulate the reader's response to and understanding of a text. For instance, the "once upon a time" formula activates the fairy tale horizon, preparing the reader for the world of gnomes, speaking mirrors, or witches whose existence is not supposed to be questioned. Sometimes texts encourage the reader to activate a certain horizon of genre expectations only to break away, interrupt, or parody the generic conventions. For instance, a text which opens with a detective investigating a murder case may break the detective story expectations by not disclosing "whodunit." But even such transgressions or violations of expectations make visible the existence of the generic "norm." In other words, for transgression to occur at all, there must be a law (code) which is recognized. In fact, few texts could be pointed out as belonging to (or written in the convention of) just one genre.

To give you an idea of the multiple issues related to the question of genre, we quote one critic's reflections:

> Does genre constitute the particular or do particulars constitute the genre? Are genres found in the texts, in the reader's mind, in the author's, or in some combination thereof? Or are they not "found" at all but, rather, devised and used? Are they "theoretical" or "historical"? Are they "prescriptive" or "descriptive"? Are they used deductively or inductively? Can we "see" them or do they hover on the hermeneutic "horizon," always potentially but never actually in view? Is their use in literary explanation inevitable? If so, should it be foregrounded? Can genres be used to explain "literariness"? Or are they the enemy of all that makes literature seem "literary"? Might they be the enemy of the reader as well, a too rigorous constraint on the interpretive act? How many genres are there? Where do they come from? How, exactly, do they work? And change? (Rosmarin, p. 7)

History

Let us look at the following two definitions of history:

> **history** 1. an account of what has happened; narrative; story; tale. 2. (a) what has happened in the life or development of a people, country, institution, etc.; (b) a systematic account of this, usually with an analysis and explanation. 3. all recorded events of the past. 4. the branch of knowledge that deals systematically with the past; a recording, analyzing, co-ordinating, and explaining of past events. (*Webster's New Twentieth Century Dictionary*, 1983 ed.)

> **history** the discipline that studies the chronological record of events (as affecting a nation or people), based on a critical examination of source materials and usually presenting an explanation of their causes. (*The New Encyclopedia Britannica*, 15th ed.)

As can be seen from the two entries, history is defined in terms of events and of a recording (telling) of these events. Thus, the word *history* is used ambiguously to describe both the past and what is written about the past. From the beginning of the Western tradition, two major tendencies are evident in the writing of history. On the one hand history is regarded as an accumulation of records; on the other it is understood as storytelling, filled with explanations of cause and effect. The historian has access to the past through its traces: documents, archival material, the testimony of witnesses, from which he/she reconstructs events. It is when the historian seeks to establish relationships between events and constructs a hypothesis that the subjective element is introduced. This subjectivity may be – and is – kept in check by the dominant paradigm of historical interpretation at a given time. That is, historians tend to write historical accounts in accordance with their culture's dominant set of beliefs and assumptions about history. These will include what counts as history, the documentation of history (what evidence of the past can be given the status of document?), the historian's role (should she/he mostly record events or should she/he offer explanations?), and the function of histories (should they evoke patriotic feelings, for instance?).

In the last two decades the question of history writing has been reconsidered along the lines of structuralist and poststructuralist thinking. Many theorists critique the claims that history belongs to the "objective" and "empirical" sciences and draw attention to the affinities between historical and fictional narratives, focusing on the role of language and the inevitability of interpretation in history writing. Michel Foucault, for instance, sees history as a set of linguistic practices which generate social and cultural activity. He criticizes the concept of total history and focuses instead on ruptures and discontinuities in history in his own "archeological" and "geneological" writing (see, for instance, his *Archeology of Knowledge*, 1972, or *The History of Sexuality*, 1980). For Hayden White, the historian writing history employs conventions which are traditionally considered literary. According to him, histories are not only about events but also about the possible sets of relationships that those events can be demonstrated to figure. These sets of relationships are not, however, immanent in the events themselves; they exist only in the mind of the historian reflecting on them. Here they are present as the modes of relationships conceptualized in the myth, fable, and folklore, scientific knowledge, religion, and literary art, of the historian's own culture. But more importantly, they are ... immanent in the very language which the historian must use to *describe* events prior to a scientific analysis of them or a fictional emplotment of them. For if the historian's aim is to familiarize us with the unfamiliar, he must use figurative, rather than technical, language.... All historical narratives presuppose figurative characterizations of the events they purport to represent and explain. And this means that historical narratives, considered purely as verbal artifacts, can be characterized by the mode of figurative discourse in which they are cast. (White, p. 94)

History, then, is one form of narrative, and as such it is subject to the same kind of analysis that other narratives are.

Ideology

Traditionally, ideology has referred to the system of ideas, values, and beliefs common to a social group and has often been equated with false consciousness. Today the term is used to signal the processes by which social subjects are formed in a given culture. The ways in which what we believe, feel, or value are linked to the reproduction of power structures in the society we live in.

In literary criticism ideology refers to a system of representations, perceptions, and images which appear to be natural and universal and which inform the text. Representations of the world in literature and other cultural artifacts participate in the construction of the world, its meaning, the role subjects are expected to play, etc. Ideological analysis in literary studies examines how textual representations of "reality" position the reader in relation to such issues as gender, race, self, class, and knowledge.

Contemporary critical theory, most notably Marxism, feminism, and new historicism, reads for subtexts of ideological formations, for the unconscious assumptions by which a society propagates its values. That is, it encourages "reading against the text," against what the text "wants" and seems to be saying. The aim is to disclose the institutional pressures and ideological formations that speak through texts and influence readers. It needs to be pointed out that although it is possible to distinguish between ruling and oppositional ideologies, even the ruling ideology is a site of conflict and struggle.

Although in the context of ideological criticism it is customary to speak of mystification and demystification, it has to be pointed out that demystification is inevitably involved in re-mystification. That is, no description or its "deciphering" is disinterested. Values, beliefs, and experiences shape both the text and the text's analysis. The critic or interpreter, just like the author, occupies some position of values and interests. In other words, it is impossible to get outside ideology.

Interpretation

Interpretation has always been an integral part of literary criticism, but whereas pre-twentieth-century criticism generally did not see interpreting the text as different from reading and understanding it, modern critics distinguish the act of reading and understanding from the act of interpreting. The term *interpretation* tends to be used for such instances of reading which uncover "hidden" meaning in a text. One of the crucial presuppositions operating in interpretation is the notion of coherence. In the words of one contemporary theorist, "An interpretation ... is a hypothesis about the most general organization and coherence of all the elements that form a literary text" (Ellis, p. 202).

The interpretation of texts is not limited to literature. Lawyers and historians, to name just two groups, are also involved in the practice of interpreting texts. In fact, interpretation has its roots in theology, or, to be more specific, in its attempts to explain biblical texts, an activity often referred to as exegesis.

A general account of the principles involved in making sense of texts has been termed hermeneutics. Crucial to this theory is the concept of the "hermeneutic circle," which refers to the following paradox: we cannot understand the text's structural and linguistic parts except in the light of the whole, and yet we can know the whole only as it is expressed in its parts. One of the important issues in theories of interpretation is the question of foundations, that is, the question whether interpretation is grounded in the text, in authorial intentions, or in the reader's interpretive strategies. Particular rules of interpretation are seen as founded on a general theory of how we understand. While earlier hermeneutics sought to reveal original meaning which was regarded as objective, today the dichotomy between the object (the text) and the subject (the interpreter) is questioned and even abandoned in many quarters. This means that rather than being concerned with understanding something (that is, with knowledge), the act of understanding in itself reveals our concept of ourselves and our being in the world. That is, it reveals the presuppositions which we bring to a text. In this sense, we are "situated," and this situatedness consists of the "prejudices" and preconceptions with which we approach the interpretation of a text.

Throughout the twentieth century, different critical schools have propagated different models of interpretation. One of the most influential has been New Criticism, which emerged as a major force in Anglo-American criticism in the 1930s and has been dominant in critical practice until quite recently. New Criticism was instrumental in establishing interpretation as a text-centered activity in search of unity in the literary artifact. Whereas New Criticism (and other pro-interpretation schools) is concerned with achieving a coherent reading of a text, much contemporary critical theory (for instance, deconstruction) instead sets out to expose these elements of a text which resist attempts to impose coherent patterns and which the texts themselves try to conceal.

Intertextuality

Two critics are generally credited with having formulated and developed the notion of intertextuality: Julia Kristeva and Roland Barthes. Kristeva used the term first in her presentation of Mikhail Bakhtin's idea of dialogism. (Hence you may hear such terms as *polyphony*, *heteroglossia*, and *dialogism* in the context of critical discussions of intertextuality. These terms, originally informing the thinking of Bakhtin, have become part of the general theoretical vocabulary.) Kristeva's understanding of intertextuality is very complex, but its gist is perhaps best summarized in her statement that "any text is constructed as a mosaic of quotations; any text is the absorption and transformation of another" (p. 66). Similarly, Barthes proposes that a text is "woven entirely with citations, references, echoes, cultural languages ... antecedent or contemporary, which cut across it through and through in a vast stereophony" (1977, p. 160).

The concept of intertextuality is variously understood in various theories. Deconstructionist theories of literature see intertextuality as an infinite play of relationships between a given text and all other texts. Intertextuality is seen as the condition of all texts, and thus it can never be fully described; it is a basic characteristic of language itself. In semiotic approaches to intertextuality texts are conceived of as made out of pieces of other texts and as such analyzable – even if never fully – in relation to other texts and other signifying practices or uses of signs in culture. Understood in this way, from the point of view of methodology, the concept of intertextuality is not radically different from the concept of influence.

Model of communication

Roman Jakobson's (1896–1982) model of the functions of language has had an enormous influence on literary theorists for the last 30 years. According to Jakobson, all acts of communication, be they written or oral, are contingent on six constituent elements which may be best presented by the following diagram:

context

message

addresser (sender) . . . . addressee (receiver)

contact

code

According to this model, all communication consists of a message sent by an addresser to an addressee. In order for the message to be transmitted, there has to be contact (physical or psychological, oral, visual, electronic, written, etc.) between the addresser and the addressee, and the message has to be formulated in terms of a code (speech, writing, cipher, etc.). The entire communicative transaction takes place in a context. The context in which the message is emitted, transmitted, and received influences its interpretation. That is, messages are always context-sensitive. Jakobson stresses that the message is not equivalent to the meaning; meaning is the function of the entire act of communication.

Each of the constituent elements of the communicative act has a corresponding function, which may be presented in the following diagram:

referential

poetic

emotive   conative

phatic

metalingual

The emotive function reflects the speaker's attitude toward the topic of his/her discourse. The conative function is centered on the receiver. The referential function privileges the informational content of an utterance. The phatic function is centered on the channel used, that is, on the contact between the sender and the receiver. The metalingual function focuses on the clarification of the manner in which the verbal code is used. Finally, the poetic function draws attention to the signifier and foregrounds the aesthetic aspect of language.

Realism

Probably the most common belief about literature is that it is a "representation of life." This belief is implicit in the term *realism*. In theories of the novel, the question of realism is central. The basic assumption in definitions of the novel is that the reader expects the presented world to be like (to reflect) empirical reality and "judges" the novel's genre by its departures from representational authenticity. Language is treated as a transparent medium. In current literary criticism this theory of imitation (or mimesis) is less popular (and regarded as less sophisticated) than the theory of realism as a narrative convention.

Realism can be defined as a term denoting a set of conventions which can be extrapolated from the "realistic" novels written in France (e.g. Honoré de Balzac) and England (e.g. George Eliot) in the period between (roughly) 1830 and 1890, and in the United States (e.g. Theodore Dreiser and Edith Wharton) at the turn of the century. Among these conventions are details about the time and place of events; representation of characters in such a way that they appear to be psychologically "full" human beings; a physical, social, and economic setting which the reader may recognize as probable; a causal arrangement of events; and a resolution or closure, that is, an end (often a marriage or a death) which is the result of the series of events and which does not leave any of the questions raised in the novel unanswered.

Although we may strive to minimize our use of figurative language and attempt to write in neutral prose, linguistic transparency is not possible, according to poststructuralist theory. As you have seen, even the language of reporting (Unit Two) and the language of historical accounts (Unit Three) are full of persuasive devices and figures of speech.

Rhetoric

The word hearkens back to the Greek word for speech, and was often found in the collocation *techne rhetorike*, which means "the art of speech" or, more generally, the skills of public speaking. Today the term is associated with the devices of persuasion as applied in either written or spoken form. Greek and Roman classical rhetoric divided the skills of persuasion into varying categories, but one of the central distinctions made was between the appeal to reason and the appeal to feeling. In relation to the latter, a defense oration in the ancient law-court, for example, was supposed to both start (the *exordium*) and end (the *preoratio*) with an appeal to feeling. In the *exordium* the speaker was expected to disarm a possibly hostile audience by means of a humorous anecdote and self-deprecating remarks. The idea that the speaker or writer must be prepared for resistance from his (or her) listeners/readers has remained basic to the concept of rhetoric ever since.

Classical theorists following Aristotle saw rhetoric as including three components, namely *invention*, the finding of topics or arguments; *disposition*, the ordering of ideas; and *style*, the choice of words, figures of speech, and syntactic and sound patterns. Units Two and Three in this book make use of these concepts when they direct attention to the ways authors select and order their material and the way they make choices among a number of possible semantic alternatives, syntactic patterns, figures of speech, and narrative devices.

All terms for classifying figures of speech, such as metaphor, metonymy, and synecdoche, derive from classical rhetoric and were considered an important part of style and its ultimate aim of persuasion. The idea of a figure of speech or trope (which means a turn or conversion away from what is taken to be a standard or literal meaning) has traditionally been associated with distortion, which in turn has been related to the issue of honesty or lying in persuasion. Socrates condemned rhetoric as the "mother of lies" because of its potential for the manipulation of an audience, and the idea of insincerity and lack of reliable meaning is still associated with rhetoric, as in the phrase "empty rhetoric." In the eighteenth century, when figures of speech were associated with the adornment of the "plain" truth, rhetoric was linked to a sometimes suspect artificiality.

Poststructuralist thinking in our period takes a radically different position and argues that all language is inherently figurative. This position is held by, for instance, Paul de Man in *Allegories of Reading* (1979) and Hayden White in *Tropics of Discourse*. In this view "rhetoric" signals undecidability of meaning. A deconstructive reading attempts to reveal those moments when what a text says seems to be contradicted by the rhetoric in which it "says" it. Such a reading attempts to show that ways of knowing are dependent on ways of saying. This critical idea and practice informs a rapidly growing body of work on the rhetoric of science, legal discourse, politics, economy, etc.

Text

In poststructuralist literary criticism and theory, the term *text* has replaced the term *work*. The terms do not refer to two different kinds of objects but to two different ways of thinking about, say, a novel or a poem. The classic notion of a *work* connotes a closed, finished, self-contained object. The critic approaches a poem or a novel as an object endowed with precise analytically isolated properties, an object which can be seen as an organism (the New Critical view) or as one which has the "stiffness ... of a crystal," in the words of the structuralist theorist Claude Lévi-Strauss. The modern notion of a *text* implies an open and infinite process of generating and subverting meaning. A novel, a poem, a play, or any other text is viewed as the result of a complex operation of interpretation based upon the critic's intertextual competence. Roland Barthes describes in detail the differences between a work and a text in his seminal essay "From Work to Text." He states that while the work "closes on a signified," the text "practices the infinite deferment of the signified ... its field is that of the signifier" (p. 158).

A text is a product of semiosis, that is, of encoding signs into "structures." Texts can be verbal, visual, aural, or kinetic. Thus, not only a poem or a novel but also a gesture, a phrase, a painting, or a meeting may be called a "text." Texts are capable of generating multiple readings and interpretations.

Suggestions for Further Reading

Below we list a few articles and books which we feel include particularly helpful discussions of the main issues in each of the nine units of this book. It is idiosyncratic in that it reflects our tastes and preferences.

Unit One

Chapman, Simon, and Garry Egger. "Myth in Cigarette Advertising and Health Promotion." In *Language, Image, Media*, ed. Howard Davis and Paul Walton. London: Basil Blackwell, 1983:166–86.

The authors offer structuralist readings of several cigarette ads (e.g. Marlboro) and discuss the techniques of creating the "health" mythology in Western culture.

Fokkema, Douwe W. "The Concept of Code in the Study of Literature." *Poetics Today* 6 (1985):643–56.

The author gives a short survey of definitions of the concept of "code" and suggests that there are at least five codes operative in literary texts: the linguistic, literary, generic, period, and idiolect. Although he defends the usefulness of the concept of code in the study of literature, Fokkema also discusses the objections of some critics regarding the applicability of the term.

Unit Two

Berlin, James A. "An Overview." In *Rhetoric and Reality: Writing Instruction in American Colleges, 1900–1985.* Carbondale, Ill.: Southern Illinois Univ. Press, 1987:1–31.

Berlin presents a useful survey of various approaches to rhetoric understood as a production of spoken and written texts. He also briefly discusses the relationship between rhetoric and poetics (the interpretation of texts).

Unit Three

Collingwood, R. G. "The Historical Imagination." In *The Idea of History.* Oxford: Clarendon, 1946:231–49.

This is a classic statement by a well-known philosopher of history on the way historians necessarily "tamper" with their sources by selection and interpolation. In this sense, Collingwood argues, "the historian is his own authority and his thought autonomous."

White, Hayden. "Interpretation in History" and "The Historical Text as Literary Artifact." In *Tropics of Discourse: Essays in Cultural Criticism.* Baltimore: Johns Hopkins Univ. Press, 1978:51–100.

In this study, the author argues that historical accounts rely heavily on figurative language as well as on the plotting devices we normally associate with fiction.

Unit Four

Culler, Jonathan. "Conventions and Naturalization" and "Poetics of the Lyric." In *Structuralist Poetics: Structuralism, Linguistics and the Study of Literature.* London: Routledge & Kegan Paul, 1975:131–88.

Drawing upon the propositions of structuralism, Culler discusses the questions of cultural *vraisemblance* and the basic conventions of reading the lyric.

Jauss, Hans-Robert. *Toward an Aesthetic of Reception* (1967), trans. Timothy Bahti. Brighton: Harvester, 1982.

In this book Jauss develops his influential theory of the "horizons of expectations." By this he means the shared set of assumptions which a given generation of readers applies to their readings of literature.

Unit Five

Said, Edward W. *Orientalism: Western Conceptions of the Orient.* Harmondsworth: Penguin, 1978:1–73.

In this classic study, Said presents the historical process of constructing the "Orient" as the other of the "Occident." The construction of Orientalism, according to Said, is predicated on the perception of the European culture as positionally superior.

Schweickart, Patrocinio P. "Reading Ourselves: Toward a Feminist Theory of Reading." In *Gender and Reading: Essays on Readers, Texts, and Contexts.* Baltimore: Johns Hopkins Univ. Press, 1986:31–62.

The essay relates feminist criticism to reader response theory, and surveys studies of the position of the woman reader in relation to the male literary canon, to women's writing, and to the reading strategies of influential male critics.

Showalter, Elaine. "The Rise of Gender." In *Speaking of Gender.* Ed. Elaine Showalter. New York: Routledge, Chapman and Hall, 1989:1–13.

This is a useful survey of the main theoretical issues of the gender studies debate of the 1980s as it applies to the study of literature. If gender criticism is to develop, Showalter argues, it is important that it extend its studies of gender construction from femininity to masculinity.

Travis, Molly Abel. "*Beloved* and *Middle Passage:* Race, Narrative, and the Critic's Essentialism." *Narrative* 2 (1994):179–200.

In the essay Travis addresses the question "What *essentially* does it mean, can it mean, to read as an African-American?" She discusses the narrative strategies of traditional slave narratives and modernist and postmodern novels through which the reader is positioned as regards race issues.

Unit Six

Clayton, Jay, and Eric Rothstein. "Figures in the Corpus: Theories of Influence and Intertextuality." In *Influence and Intertextuality in Literary History.* Eds. Jay Clayton and Eric Rothstein. Madison, Wis.: Univ. of Wisconsin Press, 1991:3–36.

This introduction to a collection of essays on influence and intertextuality offers a survey of the concept of intertextuality as it figures in the works of Kristeva, Barthes, Derrida, Riffaterre, and Foucault. The introduction also offers a brief explanation of the reasons behind the decline of the concept of influence.

Morgan, Thaïs. "The Space of Intertextuality." In *Intertextuality and Contemporary American Fiction.* Eds. Patrick O'Donnell and Robert Con Davis. Baltimore: Johns Hopkins Univ. Press, 1989:239–79.

The article gives a very useful survey of theories of intertextuality. T. S. Eliot's ideas in "Tradition and the Individual Talent" are discussed together with Harold Bloom's *Anxiety of Influence.* Morgan compares the ideas of Lotman, Bakhtin, Barthes, Kristeva, Derrida, Riffaterre, Genette, and Foucault concerning intertextuality.

Unit Seven

Chatman, Seymour. "A New Kind of Film Adaptation: *The French Lieutenant's Woman.*" In *Coming to Terms: The Rhetoric of Narrative in Fiction and Film*. Ithaca, NY: Cornell Univ. Press, 1990:161–83.

Chatman offers an interesting analysis of Karel Reisz's film based on Fowles's novel. He focuses on the interrelations between the Victorian and the modern story as rendered in Reisz's film.

Rimmon-Kenan, Shlomith. *Narrative Fiction: Contemporary Poetics*. London: Methuen, 1983.

The book is an excellent and relatively straightforward introduction to the basic concepts of narratology. Especially useful are the author's numerous references to various literary texts as illustrations of the concepts.

Wellek, René, and Austin Warren. "The Nature and Modes of Narrative Fiction." In *Theory of Literature*. Harmondsworth: Penguin, 1949:212–25.

Wellek and Warren's brief presentation of the main aspects of the narrative remains highly useful.

Unit Eight

Collini, Stefan, ed. *Interpretation and Overinterpretation*. Cambridge: Cambridge Univ. Press, 1992.

The essays in this collection offer different perspectives on the issue of criteria and constraints in interpretation. Umberto Eco, Richard Rorty, Jonathan Culler, and Christine Brooke-Rose engage in a polemics over reading praxes.

Mailloux, Steven. "Interpretation." In *Critical Terms for Literary Studies*. Eds. Frank Lentricchia and Thomas McLaughlin. Chicago: Univ. of Chicago Press, 1990:121–34.

The author briefly discusses what is to be regarded as the *object* of interpretation, the *activity* of interpreting, and what counts as a *correct* interpretation in order to focus on the issue of the politics of interpretation.

Newton, K. M. *Interpreting the Text: A Critical Introduction to the Theory and Practice of Literary Interpretation.* New York: Harvester Wheatsheaf, 1990.

Newton's book offers an excellent survey of different approaches to the question of interpretation. The author discuss the New Critical, poststructuralist, Marxist, feminist, and reader-oriented theoretical schools. He also gives an account of the "against interpretation" positions.

Unit Nine

Booth, Wayne C. *The Company We Keep: An Ethics of Fiction.* Berkeley: Univ. of California Press, 1988.

In his introduction Booth discusses the way overtly ethical and political approaches to literature challenge the formal (or aesthetic) interests in the literary text.

Connor, Steven. *Theory and Cultural Value.* Oxford: Blackwell, 1992.

In the various chapters of his book, Connor presents the discussion on value in Marxism, feminism, deconstruction, and the postmodern philosophy of Habermas, Lyotard, and Rorty, as well as in Freud and Bataille.

Smith, Barbara Herrnstein. *Contingencies of Value: Alternative Perspectives for Critical Theory.* Cambridge, Mass.: Harvard Univ. Press, 1988:esp. 1–16.

The author argues that the value of the text is dependent (contingent) on the changing values of a community, and that readers activate various potential meanings of texts in accordance with such values.

Torgovnick, Marianna. "Taking Tarzan Seriously" In *Gone Primitive: Savage Intellects, Modern Lives.* Chicago: Univ. of Chicago Press, 1990:42–72.

The essay focuses on the representation of the female and the savage. It briefly analyzes a few illustrations of Tarzan (posters, ads, book covers).

Works Cited

Adler, Jerry, et al. 1991. "Thought Police." *Newsweek*, January 14.

Agar, Herbert. 1950. *The Price of Union*. Boston: Houghton Mifflin.

Anderson, Charles R. 1960. *Emily Dickinson's Poetry: Stairway of Surprise*. New York: Holt, Rinehart & Winston.

Barthes, Roland. 1977. "From Work to Text." In *Image – Music – Text*. Trans. Stephen Heath. New York: Hill and Wang.

—. 1986. "The Discourse of History." In *The Rustle of Language*. Trans. Richard Howard. New York: Hill and Wang, 127–40.

Bateson, F. W. 1950. *English Poetry: A Critical Introduction*. London: Longman, Green and Company.

Beauvoir, Simone de. [1949] 1988. *The Second Sex*. Trans. H. M. Parshley. London: Picador.

Belsey, Catherine. 1980. *Critical Practice*. London: Methuen.

Booth, Wayne C. 1961. *The Rhetoric of Fiction*. Chicago: Univ. of Chicago Press.

—. 1988. *The Company We Keep: An Ethics of Fiction*. Berkeley: Univ. of California Press.

Brooks, Cleanth. 1951. "Irony as a Principle of Structure." In *Literary Opinion in America*. Ed. M. D. Zabel. 2nd ed. New York: Peter Smith.

Brooks, Cleanth, and Robert Penn Warren. 1943. *Understanding Fiction*. New York: Appleton-Century-Crofts.

Burroughs, Edgar Rice. [1912] 1990. *Tarzan of the Apes*. New York: Signet Classic.

Chatman, Seymour. 1990. *Coming to Terms: The Rhetoric of Narrative in Fiction and Film*. Ithaca, NY, and London: Cornell Univ. Press.

Coetzee, J. M. 1987. *Foe*. Harmondsworth: Penguin.

Conrad, Joseph. [1902] 1980. *Heart of Darkness*. New York: Signet Classic.

Corti, Maria. 1978. *An Introduction to Literary Semiotics*. London: Indiana Univ. Press.

Crosman, Robert. 1982. "How Readers Make Meaning." *College Literature* 9:207–15.

Defoe, Daniel. [1719] 1983. *Robinson Crusoe*. Oxford: Oxford Univ. Press.

Dickinson, Emily. [1929] 1957. "My Life had stood – a Loaded Gun –." In *The Complete Poems of Emily Dickinson*. Ed. Thomas H. Johnson. New York: Little, Brown and Company.

Duchamp, Marcel. 1919. *Mona Lisa: L.H.O.O.Q.*

Easthope, Antony. 1991. "Literary Value Again: A Reply to Steven Connor." *Textual Practice* 5:334–36.

Eco, Umberto. 1992. "Overinterpreting Texts." In *Interpretation and Over-interpretation*. Ed. Stefan Collini. Cambridge: Cambridge Univ. Press, 45–66.

Ellis, John M. 1974. *The Theory of Literary Criticism: A Logical Analysis*. Berkeley: Univ. of California Press.

Ewen, Edward T. 1962. "Eh-wa-au-wau-aooow." *New York Times*, September 23.

Faulkner, William. [1930] 1967. "A Rose for Emily." In *Collected Stories of William Faulkner*. New York: Random House.

— [1936] 1971. *Absalom, Absalom!* Harmondsworth: Penguin.

Fekete, John. 1987. "Introductory Notes for a Postmodern Value Agenda." In *Life After Postmodernism: Essays on Value and Culture*. Ed. and introd. John Fekete. New York: St. Martin's.

Fetterley, Judith. 1978. *The Resisting Reader: A Feminist Approach to American Fiction*. Bloomington, Ind.: Indiana Univ. Press.

Fitzgerald, F. Scott. [1925] 1968. *The Great Gatsby*. Harmondsworth: Penguin.

Fowles, John. 1969. *The French Lieutenant's Woman*. London: Jonathan Cape.

The French Lieutenant's Woman. 1981. Film director Karel Reisz. Screenplay Harold Pinter.

Garraty, John A. 1983. *The American Nation*. New York: Harper and Row.

Gelpi, Albert. 1979. "Emily Dickinson and the Deerslayer." In *Shakespere's Sisters: Feminist Essays on Women Poets*. Eds. Sandra M. Gilbert and Susan Gubar. Bloomington: Indiana Univ. Press.

Gilbert, Sandra M., and Susan Gubar. 1979. *The Madwoman in the Attic: The Woman Writer and the Nineteenth-Century Literary Imagination*. New Haven: Yale Univ. Press.

The Great Gatsby. 1974. Film director Jack Clayton. Screenplay Francis Ford Coppola.

Holtsmark, Erling B. 1981. *Tarzan and Tradition: Classical Myth in Popular Literature*. Wesport, Conn.: Greenwood Press.

Hutcheon, Linda. 1988. *A Poetics of Postmodernism: History, Theory, Fiction*. New York: Routledge.

Iser, Wolfgang. 1974. *The Implied Reader: Patterns of Communication in Prose Fiction from Bunyan to Beckett*. Baltimore: Johns Hopkins Univ. Press.

Janson, H. W. 1986. *History of Art*. 3rd ed. Expanded and revised by Anthony F. Janson. New York: Harry N. Abrams.

Kaplan, Cora. 1986. *"The Thorn Birds*: Fiction, Fantasy, Femininity." In *Formations of Fantasy*. Eds. Victor Burgin, Donald James, and Cora Kaplan. London: Methuen, 142–66.

Kristeva, Julia. 1980. *Desire in Language: A Semiotic Approach to Literature and Art*. Ed. Leon S. Roudiez. Trans. Thomas Gora, Alice Jardine, and Leon S. Roudiez. New York: Columbia Univ. Press.

Léger, Ferdinand. 1930. *Mona Lisa with Keys*.

Lodge, David. 1988. *Nice Work*. Harmondsworth: Penguin.

McCullough, Colleen. 1977. *The Thorn Birds*. London: Futura/Macdonald.

Magritte, René. 1960. *The Gioconda*.

Mansfield, Katherine. [1917] 1937. "A Suburban Fairy Tale." In *The Short Stories of Katherine Mansfield*. New York: Alfred Knopf.

Melville, Herman. [1856] 1962. "Benito Cereno." In *Billy Budd, Sailor and Other Stories*. Chicago: Univ. of Chicago Press.

Miller, J. Hillis. 1986a. "On Edge: The Crossways of Contemporary Criticism." In *Romanticism and Contemporary Criticism*. Eds. Morris Eaves and Michael Fischer. Ithaca, NY: Cornell Univ. Press.

—. 1986b. "Postscript: 1984." In *Romanticism and Contemporary Criticism*. Eds. Morris Eaves and Michael Fischer. Ithaca, NY: Cornell Univ. Press.

Mitchell, Margaret. [1936] 1993. *Gone with the Wind*. New York: Warner Books.

Morrison, Toni. 1973. *Sula*. New York: New American Library.

—. 1992. *Playing in the Dark: Whiteness and the Literary Imagination*. Cambridge, Mass.: Harvard Univ. Press.

Muller, John P., and William J. Richardson. 1988. *The Purloined Poe: Lacan, Derrida, and Psychoanalytic Reading*. Baltimore: Johns Hopkins Univ. Press.

Mulvey, Laura. [1975] 1993. "Visual Pleasure and Narrative Cinema." Reprint. In *Contemporary Film Theory*. Ed. and introduction Antony Easthope. London and New York: Longman, 111–24.

Plath, Sylvia. [1960] 1967. "Mushrooms." In *The Colossus*. London: Faber and Faber.

Radway, Janice. 1984. *Reading the Romance: Women, Patriarchy, and Popular*

Literature. Chapel Hill: Univ. of North Carolina Press.

Rich, Adrienne. [1975] 1979. "Vesuvius at Home: The Poetry of Emily Dickinson." In *On Lies, Secrets, and Silence: Selected Prose 1966–1978*. New York: Norton.

Rimmon-Kenan, Shlomith. 1983. *Narrative Fiction: Contemporary Poetics*. London and New York: Methuen.

Rosmarin, Adena. 1985. *The Power of Genre*. Minneapolis: Univ. of Minnesota Press.

Safire, William. 1991. "'Correct Thinking' on the Campus." *International Herald Tribune*, May 6.

Stonum, Gary Lee. 1989. "Cybernetic Explanation as a Theory of Reading." *NLH* 20:397–410.

White, Hayden. [1978] 1986. *Tropics of Discourse: Essays in Cultural Criticism*. Baltimore and London: Johns Hopkins Univ. Press.

Williams, William Carlos. [1934] 1938. "This is Just to Say." In *The Collected Earlier Poems of William Carlos Williams Vol. 1 1909–1939*. New York: New Directions Publishing.

Wolosky, Shira. 1984. *Emily Dickinson: A Voice of War*. New Haven, Conn.: Yale Univ. Press.

Wordsworth, William. [1800] 1972. "A Slumber Did My Spirit Seal ..." In *The Norton Anthology of English Literature*. 4th ed. New York: Norton.

Zinn, Howard. 1980. *A People's History of the United States*. London: Longman.

Index

Anders Kristensson, *An Ordinary Family*, 1991.
Copyright © Anders Kristensson. Reprinted by permission.

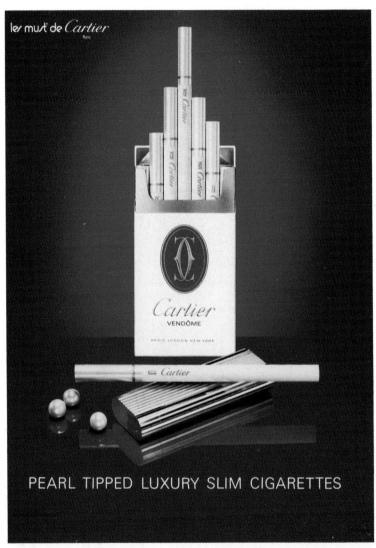

Reprinted by permission of Dunhill Tobacco of London Limited.

Reprinted by permission of Dunhill Tobacco of London Limited.

Advertisement for Kindy socks.

Publicity poster for the film "The Seven Year Itch."

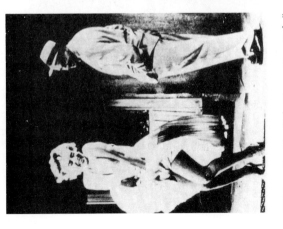

Still from the film "The Seven Year Itch."

Marcel Duchamp, *Mona Lisa: L.H.O.O.Q*, 1919.

Ferdinand Léger, *Mona Lisa with Keys*, 1930.

René Magritte, *The Gioconda*, 1960.

Daniel Spoerri, *Using a Rembrandt as an Ironing Board*, 1964.